Contents

Preface iv

Introduction: Becoming Blissful and Domestic v

1   Budgeting: Laying a
     Financial Foundation 1

2   Implementing a Budget and
     Making It Work for You 21

3   How to Cut Your Grocery Budget in Half 34

4   Become a Strategic Shopper 45

5   Menu Planning 101+ Recipes 56

6   Getting Out of Debt and Staying Out 73

7   A Great Wardrobe on a Budget 84

8   Family Night 97

9   Celebrating on a Budget 106

10   Eating Out on a Budget 122

11   A Clean Home Is a Happy Home 130

12   Keep Calm and Carry On 139

About the Author 144

Preface

Since starting my *Blissful and Domestic* blog over six years ago, I have dreamed of the moment when I would be able to sit down at my laptop and put my frugal journey into book form. What a blessing this is! For those of you who have been with me from the beginning, I thank you. Thank you for every single comment, email, thought, and prayer you sent my way. What an encouraging lot you are! For those of you who are just joining the frugal party, I welcome you! I am so excited to have you along for the ride. *Blissful and Domestic* has always been a place for creativity, encouragement, and inspiration. I pray this book will be the same.

I believe that as individuals, we are far greater than we give ourselves credit for. I feel that we should inspire and uplift others as we go throughout life. Whether you are looking for a way to get out of debt, a way to live stress-free, or a way to make ends meet, the tips and tricks in this book will help you. I didn't grow up being frugal; my journey was a gradual one. Step by step, I learned and grew. You can too! As you read the pages of this book, know that you too can live a wonderful life on less. With baby steps, you can move mountains in your life. Inch by inch, mile by mile, you can rid your family of debt and unnecessary stress. I pray you will come along with me on this journey and find your own strength along the way.

Introduction

Becoming Blissful
and Domestic

Hello, lovelies! I am so excited you are here reading this book. My sweat and tears have gone into it. My passion and faith have come along for that ride as well. I am so excited to share my frugal journey with you, and I hope that you will be blessed because of it. Before I get into the meat of the book and all the goodness it entails, I think it is only right to catch you all up on the whos and whats of my family so you understand who I am and something about the family I talk about in this book.

First of all, I am Danielle. I am a blonde-haired, blue-eyed, thirty-something mama. No, my hair is not naturally light, but I do buy the boxes of dye, so I think that qualifies me in saying the hair color is "mine" (since it is bought and paid for). I am a semi-shy gal who drools over vintage beauty and has a great love for all things chevron and damask. I am a mama who loves her family and loves to create, whether it is by writing on the blog, *Blissful and Domestic*, or transforming the house into a home. I believe that there is beauty in the simplest of things if we only search for it.

Throughout this book, you will see I have my own style of writing. I am not a fancy, schmancy writer—as if you couldn't tell by my use of the word *schmancy*. I use words like *yumminess*, *goodness*, *ginormous*, *kaboosh*, and sometimes I love to give myself a "Woot! Woot!" when I get excited. I basically talk like a teenager, even though I am thirty—er—twenty plus a few numbers. I write as if you and I were sitting down for coffee or diet cream soda on my imaginary front porch. *(Oh, how I dream of a wraparound porch with colorful rocking chairs sitting out front.)* I am a soda drinker, not a coffee drinker, so you can have coffee, and I will sip on my cream soda as we chat about all-things frugal. I like to write as if I were talking to my best friend. So remember this as you read through the pages of this book, and in the words of my redheaded Miss, we will truly become besties!

Now on to that family of mine. I married my sweet husband, Jason, in 2003. I refer to him as "the Hubbs," "Hubby," or sometimes "my green-eyed hunk." He answers to any of those. We met on a blind date in 2002, just six months after I graduated from high school. We met through some friends from the LDS Church. He called, we chatted, and then he asked me out to go bowling. He is one of the funniest people I know. He's the only person who can have my sides in stitches from laughing so hard. I honestly don't think I had ever laughed so much out loud before I met this man of mine. He had me hooked from that first hello. When we met on our blind date, things were a little different than what I thought they would be, because I already had a picture painted in my head of who this hilarious man would be. He described himself as being over six feet tall. Oh my, did he embellish with his height! He is only an inch or so taller than me (I'm five feet, seven inches). Although he fibbed a little with his appearance, we had a good laugh, and we haven't stopped since. He is my rock and supporter. He is my comic relief when times get tough and my best friend always. Being married is quite a roller coaster, but I am thankful I get to have him by my side on this ride called life.

Next in the lineup are my children. I might have seen the *Wizard of Oz* too many times or read too many children's novels by John Peterson growing up. I'm not sure. But when writing, I lovingly refer to them as "munchkins" or "littles." Why?, you may ask. Well that is what they are. They are my adorable little munchkins, who I love to the moon and back. I have two munchkins total. We lovingly call them Libby ("Miss Priss," "Little Miss," or "redheaded girl") and Keagan ("the boy," "Bubba," or "redheaded boy"). They are my world and my joy. They inspire me every single day. It is because of them and that man of mine that I chose this frugal journey. I don't regret a single day of it. This journey has made us a happier and stronger family.

Now that you know the basics, I think it is time to dive into my story, because once you know the beginning, you will see that I am not much different than you. I am imperfect (aren't we all?), struggling to become a better person each day. I have flaws (way too many to list), but despite all this, I have a love for life; my Savior; and living a provident, beautiful, and frugal life. That is what this book is all about. It's my journey to living a more frugal life, with ideas about how you can start a similar journey for yourself and your family.

I didn't start out being savvy when it came to money. In fact, it was quite the opposite. I grew up in an upper-middle class, two-story home. We went on yearly vacations to Disneyland and Universal Studios. My parents had two cars, and we were comfortable. My parents worked very hard to provide that life, but like most young adults, I forgot my parents had worked for years and years to get to that comfortable point. I was like most teenagers, focused only on the immediate gratification of life. I wanted my things, and I wanted them now. I remember many Sunday mornings spent scanning the store ads to see what was going on sale that week. I knew sales were a great way to get my mom to go shopping. She has always had the shopping bug, and when you pair the shopping bug with a good sale, the sky is the limit—or at least that is what my fifteen-year-old self thought. My mom and I were shopping buddies. We would spend our weekends hanging out and checking out whatever sales were going on that weekend. I have so many fond memories of my mom and I going shoe shopping, dress shopping, and . . . really any kind of shopping. You name it, we shopped for it. We were good at it, and we had a lot of fun. I am sure I was a big enabler, since my mom does have some shopaholic tendencies—well, a lot of them.

When I was a young teen, my mom was in her shopaholic heyday. She had many credit cards, which my dad repeatedly and dutifully cut up. I thought that credit cards could buy just about anything, including that great pair of shoes or that fabulous jacket in the store window. It was a magic card that allowed you to get something now and worry about paying for it later.

My mom's shopaholic tendencies started before I was even born. She often shares a story about what happened the first time her credit card was denied. It was Christmastime, and my older brother was just a toddler. My mom had been buying gifts and goodies. She was riding high until she went into a department store and tried to pay for her items. She got the look of shame—you know, the narrowing of eyes followed by, "Your card has been denied, Ma'am." At first, she was just distraught over being called *ma'am*. I mean, she was in her twenties, folks! Once my mom got over that shock, she realized what the store clerk was telling her. She was being informed that her magic card was not so magical after all. She couldn't understand how her card wasn't working. I guess my mom forgot that with credit cards come minimum payments. Soon after that fateful experience, my father started cutting up credit cards, and each month you would hear, "You're killing me, Kathie" when the credit card bills would arrive.

You might be wondering how she still had credit cards after my dad cut them up each month. She would just keep reapplying for them! I remember many prom seasons, searching for that perfect dress. We'd be in a department store, would find the perfect dress (like that zebra print one I rocked in 2000. You were right, Mom. It was one-of-a-kind, and it was amazing), and she would open a store credit card. I would get my fabulous dress, my mom got a new card, and my dad would get to bust out his scissors at the end of the month.

Although my mother's shopping addiction was passed down to me (much to my hubby's dismay), my parents raised two strong, independent children. My parents are amazing people. They taught me to be strong and to use my voice. They taught me to always show kindness in everything I say and do. I see both of my parents in me. My nose, big feet, and love for creating and writing come from my dad. He would spend hours creating little models out of cereal boxes. He could take simple cardboard and make it into an amazing World War II tank. From my mom, I got my eyes and my love for the written word. I would see her devour book after book while sitting out at the pool each summer. I saw that love for reading, and it rubbed off on me. Her book nerdiness is a part of me.

In 2002 when I met my husband, I was fresh out of high school and was a bit on the spoiled side. I was used to living a certain way. I was used to getting everything I asked for. I wasn't a brat—or at least not a huge one. I worked hard in school and tried to help out those around me, but I definitely loved to shop. I had worked part-time throughout high school. One of my first jobs was taking orders at the local Golden Arches. Most of my money went to green-apple body spray and bedazzled flip-flops. No joke. I was seriously obsessed with both. It wasn't until six months after I graduated high school that my life forever changed. I met my husband, and six months later he proposed.

Hubby and I married in 2003. I was nineteen. He was twenty-two. We were in newlywed bliss, spending every moment together. When we finally came back down from the newlywed clouds, real life set in, and those things we call bills started arriving in the mail. I had no clue when it came to keeping a budget and living within your means. I had never paid a bill, much less planned a grocery trip. I went grocery shopping every single week, spending over one hundred dollars a week. Why did I do that? I guess I did because my parents did. What I forgot was my parents were buying for a whole family, and I was only buying for two. They also had the extra money. I didn't. I never wrote down a grocery list. I would just go to the store and do my "wifely duty" of grocery shopping. Just so you know, "winging it" and grocery shopping should never go hand in hand—like ever—but I will talk about that later.

When I went grocery shopping, I picked out whatever looked good to me at the time and would get home only to realize that very few things actually went together. You can only do so much with Oreo cookies, fruit cocktail, chicken, and cream of wheat. (As a side note, never go shopping when you are hungry. *Never.* It's not a good idea.) Over time, Hubby had a talk with me about where our money was going. He grew up knowing that not only did you work hard for your money, but you also had to be smart with it. You had to know where all your pennies were going. His father had raised him well. This is something I am forever thankful for. He comes from a big family of six kids, so his parents had a tight budget. They made sure that their kids had all the tools needed to make good choices, especially where bills were concerned.

A few moments after Hubby gave me "the talk," I remember locking myself in the bathroom. I had some crying to do. I sat on that white-tiled bathroom floor for probably an hour. I wasn't completely keeping track of the time. (You know, because I was a hot mess, with tears all over my face. I am also not a cute crier, so my reflection in the mirror didn't help my cause either.) Eventually though, a knock came at the door. My green-eyed man was coming in, whether I thought he should or not. Remember, we were newlyweds, so I really didn't want him to see me in an unflattering way. (Little did I know, a year later we'd have a son and all thoughts of decorum would go out the window.) Eventually though, I pulled myself up off the cold tile and dried my tears. I unlocked the door and let him in. He hugged me and told me everything would be all right. He would help me. As long as we were together, we could get through anything. I believed him then, just like I do today. You can get through anything when you have the right person by your side.

My Personal Turning Point

I'd love to say that this was the last money talk Hubby had to give me, but it wasn't. I was bad—really bad—when it came to budgeting.

And the really tough times hit when he was serving his second tour of duty in Iraq as a member of the US Army. While he was in Iraq, I was left to run the family finances by myself. He had tried to teach me the basics before he left. I would tell him, "Yeah, yeah, I got this." But in actuality, I didn't. I was overwhelmed. I had two little munchkins to take care of, and my husband was gone. I was lonely. I went shopping way too often. I went grocery shopping, even when I didn't need to, because I was bored and looking for a way to get out of the house. Hubby would ask me if everything was okay. I consistently told him everything was fine. Then one day it wasn't.

I was constantly dipping into our savings to cover our checking account. I was late on bills and overdrafting like it was going out of style. I had ignored the problem for far too long. I remember when hubby called from Iraq. He was angry and confused. He didn't understand why I was lying about our finances. He wanted to know why I kept telling him everything was okay when it wasn't. I needed help, but I was allowing my pride and embarrassment to prevent me from seeking it. He placed many calls from that desert, grilling me on the way I was spending. I had a problem, and it was a big one.

Then my husband had an epiphany. He had been watching a news program and had heard someone mention *America's Cheapest Family*.[1] Annette and Steve Economides were a one-income family, making it work with five kids. They had a plan, and it was working for them. Hubby encouraged me to check their book out at the library. I was at an all-time low, so I had to do something. He was at his wit's end. He was too far away to hold my hand through the process.

I found the book at my local library. I don't think I have ever felt so inspired reading a book—apart from the Good Book, of course. I devoured the book in a day, taking notes as I went along. I knew that God wanted something better for me. I mattered to Him, and living paycheck to paycheck—constantly stressed over finances—was not what He wanted for me. He didn't want me spending each month arguing with my husband over bills. He wanted us to be a happy, forever family. He had heard my prayers, pleading for guidance, and He had delivered just that. Little by little, I started implementing the tips and tricks in the book, while putting my own spin on them. During the following weeks, Hubby and I talked about what I was learning. We made a budget over the phone and talked about all of our spending. Over time, I became less embarrassed. I stopped justifying and began accepting responsibility for the things I had done. I realized that I was spending because I was sad. I was letting the fact that I missed my husband consume my thoughts. I was filling a void with shopping.

Why do I tell you all this? Because I want you to know I was once there. I have not always been savvy with money. I struggled, I shopped, and I dug myself a hole—a fairly big one. Over time, I was able to dig myself out. We all have the ability to put down that shovel, stop digging that hole, and climb out. I did it, and so can you!

Immediately, my marriage was better. We were finally on the same page when it came to our finances. There was no longer a spirit of contention in our home. Boy, did that feel good. We weren't arguing anymore. *Hallelujah!* It was a good day when after that first month of choosing to change, I saw we were in the black. I had no overdraft charges. I literally shouted for joy and gave myself a "Woot! Woot!" It was glorious, I tell you! Absolutely glorious! I had made a plan, stuck to it, and my family was being blessed for it. In the words of my sweet husband, "It was good. Real good."

Slowly but surely, our debt burden lessened. We paid off our car (best day ever). I still remember sending in that last check. I don't know if I had ever smiled so big. I had pulled myself up off that tile floor and had done something about our finances. I took control of my family's financial future. In fact, I gave us a future because I chose to do something better. We cannot sit idly by, blaming the world for our problems. We must stand up for ourselves, our families, and our dreams. When we put action into our dreams, so many great things can happen. I learned that you can take control of your family's happiness. When we choose to free ourselves from the burdens that financial distress can cause, we can become more joyful people!

Principles for Getting Your Life on Track

Throughout this book, you will see a few recurring themes: avoiding debt like the plague, being conscious of your spending, living below your means, and embracing a frugal lifestyle. They are essential to your frugal journey, and when mastered, they will lay the groundwork for an amazing financial future where you will have more freedom. Who wouldn't want that?

Avoid Debt like the Plague

Just like *America's Cheapest Family*, I am a huge supporter of avoiding debt like the plague. We all know what a plague is right? It is an infection that causes continual turmoil, stress, and trouble. A plague can cause devastation in an instant. It spreads, hurting not only ourselves but also those around us. This is very similar to debt. When you allow yourself to go into debt, you are allowing an infection begin to fester in your finances. When left untreated, it will wreak havoc. It can completely disable you and hurt those around you. I have seen many families become disabled by their financial choices. Our financial choices affect not only ourselves but our families as well.

The overuse of credit also lowers your standard of living. When we choose to use credit to pay for expenses, we are overextending ourselves. This is something I learned firsthand. After spending freely, you eventually have to make payments on whatever you bought. You are essentially using today's money to pay for yesterday's desires. Doing this leaves you short today, since it takes away from the money you need now. This can set off a vicious cycle of events. Using today's money to pay for yesterday's wants can make it harder to pay today's bills. See the cycle? It can keep going, leaving you a stressed and behind financially. Be cautious. Buying things on credit can send you into a downward spiral faster than you think. If you *are* in debt, know there's a way out. That light at the end of the tunnel is not as far away as you think. Through hard work, most people can pull themselves out of debt in less than eighteen months. There's hope, and I will show you how!

Be Conscious of Your Spending

This is for everyone, regardless of income level. It is essential to be aware of the way your money is being spent. We must know where every single penny is going. We have to be aware of what is going on in our lives. You will read this a lot in this book, but it is essential! You cannot sit idly by as life happens. You need to stand up and take control. No one is going to come save you. You need to save yourself. When I was sitting on that bathroom tile, crying my newlywed eyes out, I knew that I had to get up. I had made poor financial choices, but I could make new, better choices. Never forget that we can change today by choosing right.

We live in a world that tells us, "Don't worry about it." But putting things on the back burner only allows problems to fester. Trust me, lovelies! I spent a lot of time trying to ignore my financial problems, but guess what? They only got worse. We can't ignore our problems. We have to face them, no matter how ugly they may seem. If we don't, who will?

Living Below Your Means

Living below my means is one financial rule that has allowed me to stay on budget continually and not go back to my old overdraft habits. Living below your means simply means spending less than you earn, and it is accomplished by creating a budget that will work for your family. I will go over this in chapters one and two. I will show you how to create a budget and how to set aside money each month to cover your expenses in advance. We live in a fast-paced world. The new goodie is always being outshined by an even newer one. It is easy to get out of control keeping up with all the hype. A budget is a tool to keep you on track and account-able for all of that spending you do. It will also help you to be conscious of how you spend your money. (See how all these themes coincide with one another?) "Budgeting is the cornerstone of family finances."[2] It is the essential piece to the puzzle that will make all those plans you create as a family a reality. When you have a budget set, living below your means becomes achievable. Living below your means entails much more than just paying the bills with cash instead of credit. Throughout this book, you will see that there are many ways to cut spending and save your family money. This will free up money you didn't even know you had, which means more fun things for you and your family to do! Are you excited yet? I know I am!

Embrace a Frugal Lifestyle

Before I go on, we need to hit the pause button. I need to get one thing straight: being frugal is not the same as being cheap. *Cheap* is a yucky word. *Frugal* is a happy word. Being frugal is making the most out of what you have. It is stretching your dollar as far as it can go. It is being resourceful and thinking outside the box. It is changing the way you see things so you start to see them in a whole new light. For me, being frugal has become a game I play. I am a smidgen competitive. Because of that, I want to win at this game. I want to get the biggest prize at the end of the day. I want that obnoxious stuffed purple elephant you always try to win at that children's pizza arcade but never have enough tickets for. That is the type of prize I want to win. For me, the money and time I save each day is that big, fluffy elephant. That is pure victory for me, folks! Don't be jealous though. You too can win your own metaphorical stuffed elephant. Naysayers think embracing a frugal life is a waste of time, but I strongly disagree. Every chapter in this book will offer you tidbits of advice that will help your family win that stuffed elephant every time. As you celebrate your own frugal victories, you will see that these principles do work. You can do it!

Make This Book Work for You

Will everything in this book work for you? Maybe not at first, but eventually you will be able to learn a new way to live and revel in it. Do not try to do everything at once. That would be overwhelming, and you will likely feel defeated right from the start. No one wants that. Pick one thing to work on. Once you have that thing down, move onto something else. It takes about thirty days to create a new habit. Keep this in mind while you try out new things. Give yourself a little grace, and know you may fall, but you can pick yourself up and try again. Celebrate small victories. If you are paying off debt, celebrate each time you add a little extra to that monthly payment. It is awesome that you are making a plan, sticking to it, and seeing that aggregated debt get lower and lower. If you are starting out a budget for the first time, celebrate after you get through a whole month of sticking to it. That is amazing, and you deserve to give yourself a "Woot! Woot!" Let yourself know you are doing a good job. Let your spouse know he or she is doing a good job if you are doing this as a team. Celebrating is not going out and spending money, but it is recognizing that you are making changes—changes that will be for the better.

I have given much thought to the organization of this book. The chapters in this book are organized by level of importance. I start with creating a budget and implementing it because it truly is the cornerstone of your financial life. For me, creating a budget was what started the frugal wheels in motion. Following those first chapters are three chapters on grocery shopping and menu planning—two very important things for everyone to learn. For most people, the grocery bill is one expense that can be cut dramatically during the first month of frugal living. By planning and shopping smart, you will save money. The first month that I shopped on a budget, I cut our grocery bill in half. I couldn't believe the money I saved. I can't wait to show you how to save too! As you explore this book, I suggest going through with a highlighter. Highlight the ideas that stand out to you. Write your thoughts in the margins. Make this book your new "how-to" book. I pray you will be able to glean much from the words on these pages. These are the tried-and-true tips that have helped my family, and I hope they will help yours as well.

I won't lie to you and say that everything in this book is easy. Some things I suggest may seem radical, but don't be too quick to shut this book and chuck it across the room. Allow the ideas to sink in. Mull them over for a bit. In the words of my dad, "Allow it to get happy." Sometimes those crazy ideas are exactly the answers we are looking for; we just need to take the time to digest them and then see how we could make them work in our own lives.

How do I recommend reading this book? You can just dive in and read it cover to cover, you can jump from chapter to chapter to deal with whatever needs you have at the time, or you can use it as reference manual. With any method you choose, there are hundreds of savings tidbits throughout to guide you on your frugal journey. I have also included testimonials from readers of my blog, more ideas from me on how to save your family time and money, and thoughts from readers on ways they save their family money too. We can all inspire one another to live beautifully on less.

Everything in this book is something I do personally. These tips have saved my family hundreds of dollars every single year. These are the same tips and tricks that have helped thousands of *Blissful and Domestic* blog readers change their lives as well. I am passionate about families, budgeting, and living a beautiful life on less. Come along for the journey with me. I know that, at the end, you too will be able to live a more happy, beautiful life.

NOTES

1. Steve Economides and Annette Economides, *America's Cheapest Family Gets You Right on the Money: Your Guide to Living Better, Spending Less, and Cashing in on Your Dreams* (New York: Crown Business, 2007).

2. Ibid., 4.

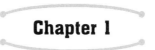

Chapter 1

Budgeting

Laying a Financial Foundation

You made it through the introduction, which means you are in. You are in for making a change that can help better your life. Are you stoked? I know I am!

Have you ever heard the song about the wise man and the foolish man? I remember learning this one at church. My mom would curl my hair and dress me up in a lace floral number, and together with the rest of my family, we ventured off to church.

The song itself is about the gospel of Christ and what we build our foundations in life on, but I think it has some merit when talking about frugal living as well. The song goes as follows:

The Wise Man and the Foolish Man

1. The wise man built his house upon the rock,
    The wise man built his house upon the rock,
    The wise man built his house upon the rock,
    And the rains came tumbling down.

2. The rains came down, and the floods came up,
    The rains came down, and the floods came up,
    The rains came down, and the floods came up,
    And the house on the rock stood still.

3. The foolish man built his house upon the sand,
    The foolish man built his house upon the sand,
    The foolish man built his house upon the sand,
    And the rains came tumbling down.

1

4. The rains came down, and the floods came up,
    The rains came down, and the floods came up,
    The rains came down, and the floods came up,
    And the house on the sand washed away.[1]

In this song, the water symbolizes the things that happen in life. Life can bring some heavy storms our way. The strength of our foundation will affect how well we endure those storms. I'd like to say that the weather in life will always be clear and sunny, but it will not. There will be times of thunder and lightning. There will be times of great rain. We will all be hit by bad weather. Sometimes we may feel like the wise man and other times we may feel like the foolish man, depending on how prepared we were for that storm. The important thing is that we have control over whether we are wise or foolish.

Budgets are personal, and no two budgets are the same. As long as you are spending less then you make, you are doing all right in my book. Take the tips throughout this chapter and this book, and make them work for you. You never know what money you could be saving until you create a budget that works for your family.

Why Making a Budget Is Important

Your budget is your lifeline in your frugal journey. It will be the foundation you build for yourself and your family. If you do not know where your money is going, then you cannot know whether you are living a self-reliant life or a life where you are digging yourself further into a hole of debt. The Economides hit the nail on the head when they described what a budget is in their first book. They said that "a family budget isn't like a New Year's Resolution, written once and then stashed away on some shelf to gather dust. And it's not like some business budgets, based on projections and then reevaluated six months later. An effective family budget is a live, functioning tool, continually updated, consulted, and adjusted as needs change."[2] A budget keeps you on track, while controlling the amount of money you spend. It is personally tailored to your family's needs.

You work hard to support yourself and your family. Because of that, wouldn't you like to know where all of your money is going? Having a budget takes the questioning part out. Having a plan written down lets you know where every cent is being used. It also tells you if you have enough coming in to support everything going out.

Budgeting is a plan that helps you make the best use of your income and savings. Budgeting is absolutely for everyone, regardless of the amount of money you make. It will help you have a plan in the way you spend your money. You may be surprised at what happens when you put your money and the way you use it down on paper. For most, this is an eye-opening experience. I know it was for me.

When I was a newlywed, and Hubby had his first finance talk with me, I couldn't believe what I had spent my money on. I had never really given it much thought. I was blissfully unaware. Once it was down on paper in black and white, I didn't like what I saw. I could no longer stay in my world of lollipops and rainbows. I couldn't hide from the truth or make excuses anymore. It's hard to hide when the truth is right there staring back at you. I hadn't been aware of the way I was spending my money because I never took the time to sit down and plan everything out. Once it was written down, it was a whole new ball game. I knew I couldn't hide behind my own ignorance anymore. I had to be accountable for the way I was spending. Having a budget is what helped me get things on track and moving in the right direction.

Budgeting Myth Buster

Very few people are educated in household finances. Most of us are given little instruction and are simply told "good luck" as we venture out into the world on our own. But managing household finances isn't much of a mystery. Anyone can learn how. Neither my husband nor I have degrees in finances. We are everyday people who found a way to manage our money. We learned that through writing everything down and being accountable for what we spent, we could make a big difference in our finances.

Now, I know there are a lot of budgeting myths out there. Some you may be thinking of one right now as you read this book. But I have a surprise for you: these myths are false. They are mental roadblocks we put up to justify why we don't budget. Here are a few of the ones I hear the most. Some I even said myself once upon a time.

Myth #1: "My family doesn't make enough money to budget."

False! No matter your family's income, you make enough to budget. There are ways to stretch even the smallest of budgets to make it work for your family. There was a time when my family lived on $14,000 a year. Hubby was a full-time student. It was hard, but we managed.

Myth #2: "Our income is not consistent enough to make a budget."

I hear this a lot from people who have jobs where work hours fluctuate depending on the time of year and commission compensation. Budgeting is the one thing that will help you plan for those months when you have a smaller income or the times when that commission check is not as big as usual. Budgeting will help you plan for that rainy day. It will give you peace of mind and security.

Myth #3: "I won't do it! A budget is too restrictive."

I strongly disagree. I have lived with a budget and without one. Trust me, living with one is so much nicer. Less stress and fewer fights with that hubby of mine. Win-win!

Myth #4: "I don't need to write it down. I have it all in my head!"

This one makes me laugh because I use to say the same thing. But guess what? My memory is not nearly that good, and I am betting neither is yours. Writing it down puts it into perspective. When we keep it all in our noggin, we forget how much we are actually spending. When we write it down, there is no more guessing or saying, "I think I have enough money for this." When we see it on paper, we know.

If you can put these myths to rest and realize there is a way to live a beautiful life on less, then you will be able to do just that. Will it take a bit of time and dedication to get started? Absolutely. But once you are on that frugal path, it is amazing to see how things become second nature. The more that you practice budgeting, the easier it will become.

It is kind of like learning to drive a car. Do you all remember when you learned? My dad was the one who taught me. When it came to driving, I wasn't sure how he was going to teach me. Would he yell? Would he laugh? I wasn't quite sure. I remember the first time I got behind the wheel. I was not like most teenagers, raring to go. I was nervous. I was going to be behind the wheel of a huge hunk of metal. Oh my! My stomach was full of butterflies. My dad took me to an empty school parking lot, and that is where I learned to drive. For months, we spent Saturday mornings practicing in that parking lot. He had me do circles, go straight, and even practice the dreaded parallel parking. I hated that! As I gained confidence, we ventured out to the road leading home from the school. Each weekend, he taught me a little bit more. My confidence grew, and it started becoming second nature. I no longer had to remind myself, "Put your blinker on. You are going to turn." I just did it. That is how your journey with budgeting will be. At first it will take a bit of work. You will have to plan and remind yourself. You are learning a new way to do things, so you will have a small learning curve. Once you start picking up momentum though, no one will be able to hold you back. You will be like that teenager who finally gets to hit the gas pedal and venture onto the highway. You will become a confident, frugally blessed individual.

Money and Your Emotions

Sometimes I think it is very easy to forget that we are human, and because we are human we tend to do things because of the emotions we are feeling at the time. We are emotional beings—some a little more than others. We can be upset with the guy in that red sports car who cut us off on the freeway, excited that we finally got that job, or heartbroken because of love lost. All of these events create strong emotions, and strong emotions sometimes dictate the way we handle our finances.

I once worked with a lady who was suffering from loss. Her husband had died suddenly, and she was understandably shaken. As time went on, she didn't deal with the grief. She used shopping as an emotional release. This was not a good habit. To start off, she still felt great sadness because shopping was only a temporary high. The grief was still waiting for her after the purchases had been made and the credit card bills arrived in the mail. She was digging herself into a huge hole of debt. Because of the emotions she was going through, her finances were suffering. It wasn't until she realized why she was spending and not budgeting that she was able to make a change.

Now, I am not qualified to help heal emotional wounds, but what I can tell you is that our emotions can drive us to do all sorts of things. I know because I have been there. When my hubby was deployed to Iraq, I was devastated. I missed him so much. I was scared he might not come back from that desert. Because of that, I used shopping as a salve for my emotional wounds. It was my way to cope with what was going on in my life. But shopping brought me only temporary happiness. It didn't fix the hurt I was carrying. It only masked it temporarily. I had to face those feelings and make some changes in order to feel lasting happiness. Some unhealthy spending habits stem from deep feelings caused by unmet needs, poor parental examples regarding money management, or other influences. Both men and women need to examine their own feelings toward money. Ask yourself why you are spending the way you are spending. Failing to identify and resolve these fundamental issues can keep a family in financial chaos for years.

I also see this type of emotional spending in marriages. Spending money can become a power struggle. A person may say, "Well, if she's going to buy a dining set, then I want a new truck." Spending out of anger or hurt is not good either. It can cause relationships to crumble. Being aware of why we spend will allow us to see how we can fix the problem. Emotional wounds hurt, but I promise that knowing where you stand financially and having control over your spending will bring you comfort and peace. It will bring you more security than you can imagine. It will bring greater unity into your marriage.

Step 1: Make an Initial Budget

When learning to budget, one of the first things you must do is distinguish between the wants and needs of your family. Realistic, workable budgets result when people agree to provide carefully for their needs and show self-discipline and patience as they seek to provide for the wants of themselves and their families. You may want to buy that new pair of shoes, but you really need to pay that water bill first. Make sense? To distinguish between wants and needs, you must write it all down. I am a big fan of pen and paper. I am often found with either a notebook or clipboard with paper on it. I write everything down. It keeps me organized. My eighth-grade English teacher would be so proud of my note-taking abilities! They have greatly improved since my teen years. The more we see our finances in black and white, the better off we will be.

Whether you keep a budget via a software program, a spreadsheet on your computer, a scrap piece of notebook paper, the back of your son's spelling test, or a phone app, it's important to do it. Start by making a list of every single bill you *have* to pay each month. Make sure it is a "need to pay" bill. Getting your nails done, putting the children in dance classes, or having that movie date night are not needs, so they should *not* be included in your initial budget. Your initial budget is to see first if you have enough money to pay for all of the basic necessities.

Sample Budget

It's pretty simple for most people who are honest with themselves to distinguish between wants and needs. We *need* a safe place to live.

We *need* electricity for power. We *need* water to drink and food to eat. These are needs. Write out all of your "need to pay" bills on your sheet of paper and add it up. Now add up your monthly income. See if your monthly expenditures outstrip your monthly income. If they do, then changes need to be made, and I'll help you discover those. If your income leaves you a bit of wiggle room, then you can budget in things like dates, family outings, extracurricular activities for the kids, and so on. I talk more about this in chapter two. Writing everything down really puts it into perspective. It allows you to see exactly what you have to pay for each month and how much you're earning. Knowing where every dime is going will make a huge difference to your frugal journey. Make your hard work be for something good and your long hours at the office mean something.

When a budget is prepared, it is something the whole family should be involved in. If you are a couple, then both parties should be involved in the budgeting and the planning part of your frugal journey. Having both partners involved is key in a successful budget. If you have children, you can explain to them what a budget is and how it will benefit the family as a whole. Remember that we do not always give our children enough credit. They understand a lot more than we think. Children are not limited by their capacity to learn, but rather by our ability to teach them. Include them. Living on a budget affects the whole family.

Couples must view themselves as partners, each with an equal voice. One of the main causes for arguing in relationships is finances. If you could alleviate that stress, you would have a stronger, more loving relationship. Including both sides in all aspects of budgeting is essential for successfully finding solutions to financial problems.

Step 2: Sit Down and Start Communicating

Communicating effectively is crucial. When discussing a budget and reviewing expenses, be sure that the discussions are just that—discussions. If both parties are talking out of love and not hate, then you will be able to come up with a better budget and plan for your family.

If you are the one who has been overspending, now is the time to fess up. It is hard to admit that you were not smart with your money, but the more that you admit your limitations, the better able you will be to find solutions. Problems arise when one spouse makes financial decisions without consulting the other. Gordon B. Hinckley once said, "There would be fewer rash decisions, fewer unwise investments, fewer consequent losses, fewer bankruptcies if husbands and wives would counsel together on such matters and unitedly seek counsel from others."[3]

When I was a young wife with little financial background, I had to learn some hard lessons. Hubby and I had gotten our first joint checking account. We got our fancy new debit cards. I thought they were the answer to any spending problem I had. If I needed groceries, I could just swipe my card. If I needed to get a new pair of shoes, I could swipe my card. Pretty soon, I was in a pickle. When Hubby confronted me about these charges, it was my initial response to get defensive and cry. I shut down. I was embarrassed by what I had done. I wanted to justify that I needed those shoes. I believe my exact words were, "I don't have a pair of blue wedges, so I needed them!" Soon, I had an excuse for every single thing I bought. Justifying my spending was causing stress in my marriage. I love my green-eyed hunk. I didn't want to spend our time as newlyweds arguing. Our initial refusal to consult one another about financial concerns quickly started to impact our marriage. Because we didn't communicate, he'd spend money, and then—thinking that there was plenty in the account—I'd spend it too, and a nasty pile of overdraft fees accumulated.

We were each doing our own thing, hoping that if we ignored the money issues we were having, we would prevent arguments. Those problems just accumulated, which led to bigger arguments. You cannot brush your financial problems under a rug to deal with another day. Don't let those issues fester! You have to communicate with one another. It is the only way to make sure that you are both on the same page.

If you are an individual making a budget, you will follow the same steps. Be honest with yourself about your spending. Don't shroud yourself in justifications. Be honest, and you will be able to see where your budget has room for improvements.

Step 3: Take Account of Your Checking and Savings

Most families can reduce some of their expenditures with a little resourcefulness and accountability. Once you have made your initial budget and know all the "need to pay" items, go through your bank account for the past few months. Going back three months is best. Doing this allows you to compare the number on the "need to pay" sheet you just made to a three-month average of what you are actually spending.

I can still remember the first time I went through my bank account and wrote down exactly what I was spending. I went through three months of spending, writing everything down on a piece of notebook paper. Line after line, I was filling up my sheet. I couldn't believe it when I needed to add more sheets because of all the times I had spent money. My mind was blown. I hadn't realized that I was eating out that much. I was only getting happy meals for my redheads as a special treat, but those special treats were making quite a dent in our budget. I also added up every time I ran into the store for a few items. Those random trips throughout the week added up to hundreds of dollars. Being able to see this in black and white made a huge difference.

Once you have gone through your checking, do the same for your savings. See if you have been transferring funds from your savings to cover expenses in your checking.

Cutting the Fat

Now that your initial budget is ready to go, it is time to customize it and see where you can *cut the fat*. Whether you've made your budget and realized that your outgoing amount far outweighs your incoming amount or whether you see you have some wiggle room, there are things you can do to help yourself stay in the black and possibly save money each month as well!

If your budget is in the red, the first plan of attack will be something I call *cutting the fat*. Crunching those numbers is key to making sure that you are living within your means. When you're not, one simple option is to reexamine your expenses and make some sacrifices.

Cutting Cable

You do not need cable television to live. It is a shock to some, but it is a fact. Sometimes we all feel like we need a little bit of TV time to unwind, but cable TV service is a luxury with a capital *L*. This should be one of the first things to go if you are living in the red. Many networks offer current-season shows on their websites. This allows you to stay current on all your favorite shows without paying a dime. With companies like Netflix and Hulu taking center stage, you can also pay less money and still watch all of your favorite shows. If you are paying for cable television, you're paying for hundreds of stations you never watch. You are literally paying to channel surf each month. Just think what you could do with that extra money (not to mention the extra time you'd save) if you nixed cable.

Even if your budget has you in the black at the end of the month, cutting cable is still something to think. Once it's gone, you'll start to make more intentional media choices. Interestingly, you'll also have more control over what your family is watching and when you watch it than you ever had before.

Cutting the Cord . . . the Phone Cord, That Is

Now on to the phone. If you have not gotten rid of your landline, I am here to tell you that this is the twenty-first century, and now is the time to cut the phone cord. Cell phones are a great way to stay connected to your family and friends and not be tied down to a home phone. Check with different cell phone plans and see what you can do to save money. There's no need to be loyal to any particular company. Find a plan that works for you and your budget. Whether it is going with a big-name cell phone company or a prepaid phone, you will save money by committing to using only a cell phone, so cut the cord and the landline with it.

If you already have a cell phone, check and see if there are ways to save. I recently worked with a lady who had been on the same cell phone plan for six years. She was paying over eighty dollars per month, but she did not get any of the perks that are becoming standard with phones, such as texting and web access. She'd never questioned whether her provider had something better to offer. Once she called her phone provider, she was able to get on a new plan, pay less, and have more fun perks to go with her phone. It never hurts to ask questions and update plans. It could save you a lot of money.

Shop around for Insurance

Every year, Hubby and I like to reevaluate to see if our current insurance plans are working for our family's needs and budget. There is no need to be loyal to a company if it is hurting your budget. If you can find another provider that will give you the same coverage for less money, then go for it. This is a simple way to cut costs and save a bit more each month.

Downsizing

Another way to cut the fat is to downsize. Downsizing applies to cars, homes, and overall lifestyle. Look at your car and see how it is affecting your family's budget. You may need a car to get to work, but you don't need a luxury vehicle. A fancy sports car will not get you to work any faster than a four-door sedan. What about that gas-guzzling SUV you think you need? Take time to evaluate your automobile expenses and see if it's time to trade for a smaller, more economical car until you have your budget under control.

When Hubby and I were first starting out, we had a used Daewoo. My parents gave it to us after we were married. It was completely paid for, and it didn't cost much to insure. That silver four-door got us through many trips back and forth to visit family and brought two redheads home from the hospital. It was a tough little car, until one fall evening when it died. It made it to Vegas for one final move back to the desert, and then it died right there in the driveway. We had run that poor silver car to the ground, but it had served us well. We needed a new car, and I wanted a van. We didn't look at mileage, gas prices, or anything. I had always wanted a van, with the hopes of filling it with many more redheads one day, so that's what we got. We kept that car for years and even paid it off, but eventually the fact that we had to drop sixty dollars or more every time we wanted to fill it up got to us. We ended up saving for a newer car that was more gas efficient. We saved $12,000 and made a huge down payment on a four-door, gas-friendly hybrid. We love our little "rocket ship," as my brother-in-law calls it. It costs less than thirty dollars to fill the tank. Who could ask for anything more? Downsizing helped our family save.

Purchasing a new car may not be in the cards right now for you, but there are other things you can do to save when it comes to your car. Be purposeful about where you drive. When we had our gas-guzzler, we made sure to combine trips when we ran errands. (We still do this now with our hybrid.) We wanted to make sure that every single mile was used wisely. By doing that, we were able to stretch our gas budget further. We set a budget for gas and stayed within that budget. There were a few times we had to say no to going out with friends because our gas was low, but we had a budget to stick to. When that happened, we would just invite friends to our house so we didn't have to drive.

Downsizing can also apply to the type of home we live in. Homes are getting bigger and bigger, which means they cost a lot more to run and maintain. I recently worked with a family who wanted to learn how to budget and make their income work for their family. They had been living well beyond their means for years and knew that something needed to change. They were renting a house that was larger than what their small family needed. They had stretched themselves because they were "keeping up with the Joneses." Once they realized that they could spend less money living in a smaller house, they chose to downsize. It helped them live within their means and was cheaper to maintain because the utilities on a smaller house were considerably lower than they were on a large house. This family then used the money they saved to slowly get themselves out of debt.

Downsizing can be beneficial to you and your family. All you have to do is make those hard decisions that will help you and your budget stay in the black. Make sure that the choices you are making today are getting you where you want to be tomorrow. Downsizing your lifestyle may be one of the hardest parts of economizing, because it means finding a new way to do things. It may mean that you don't eat out or shop at expensive stores anymore. Look at your life, the way you spend your money, and see where you can downsize. What can you cut down on or cut out completely to make the numbers crunch?

Other important methods of cutting the fat are eliminating eating out and cutting down on the grocery bill. These two steps are so important, I've devoted an entire chapter to each, so don't forget to review those chapters.

Have you ever met anyone who said he or she was happy to be in debt? No, you haven't. There's a reason for that. Make a budget and stick to it. You and your family will be happier for it.

Pay Attention to Your Utilities

One thing I get asked about often is what to do about utility bills. Depending on where you live, you may find your gas bill is astronomically high in the winter while your cooling bill reaches its all-time high in the summer. No matter what the case is, there are a few things you can do. When seasonal changes to your utility use are out of whack, your budget can get out of whack too. Luckily, there are a few things you can do to help.

The first thing you can do is to plan ahead for it. If you know that your electric or gas bill will be higher in an upcoming season, start putting away some money for it now. Add a utilities section to your budget so you can put a little bit away each month. Putting away twenty-five dollars a month is a lot easier than paying one lump sum. Plan ahead and save yourself a lot of stress.

Another thing you can do is leave that thermostat alone. In the winter, keep it at sixty-eight degrees, and in the summer, keep it at seventy-eight degrees. Using a programmable thermostat can help to have the temperature adjusted when you're not at home. No need to cool down a house if you're not there to enjoy it. This is the same for the winter. Don't set your thermostat higher when you turn it on, thinking it will warm you up faster. It won't and will only leave you with an unnecessary expense.

You can also invest in some ceiling fans. They will cool you down and stop you from relying on that air conditioner so much. Swapping out your air conditioner for a swamp cooler works too! We use a swamp cooler, and it saves us a ton. Where most of our neighbors have electric bills in the high two hundred dollars, we sit comfortably at less than ninety dollars a month. Research the options for heating and cooling in your area.

When your bills come in the mail or when you pay them online, look at the consumption. This will let you see how much you used in the month compared to last month. Recently, Hubby was looking at our water bill and noticed that it was a bit higher than normal. He wasn't quite sure why it had increased, so he started poking around our home and checking things out. Upon his inspection of the pipes in our bathroom, he found a small leak. He was able to fix a problem before it became more serious. Our utility bills can tell us a lot about what is happening in our home, so pay attention. You might just catch a problem before it escalates.

Teaching Our Children Needs vs. Wants

Now that you're going to cut the fat, how do you explain it to those children of yours? Start by being honest and direct with them. Often, we shield our children from life. When things are rough, we try to keep it from them because we don't want them to see that Mom and Dad are having a hard time. I think we are doing a great disservice to them. So many great lessons can be taught if you go through hard times as a family. When Hubby got back from Iraq, he became a full-time student. He was going to school, which (thankfully) the military paid for, but our income was cut drastically. We received only a fraction of what he used to get when he was a full-time military member. We explained this to the kids in words they'd understand. Daddy was not making as much, so that meant we had to learn to live in different ways. As a family, we needed to learn the difference between wants and needs. This was not just one lesson we taught them. Kids have to be reminded and taught over and over. Even adults need this repetition from time to time. If we were at a store and they wanted a new toy, I would ask them if they thought it was a need or a want. This helped put it into perspective for them. I ask myself the same thing when I shop.

If our children are able to see us go through a trial and handle it with grace and bravery, they will do the same. They are little sponges, walking around and soaking up what is around them. If they see us struggle but get through with our heads held high, they will do the same. It is one of the most important lessons we can teach those sweet spirits we've been blessed to raise.

Work Together

When you all work together and display a great amount of teamwork, you will thrive as a family. You will see the totals in your accounts and work together as a team to get them balanced. For my hubby and I, it is great bonding time. We pick a time when we know the littles will not interrupt us. For my family, that usually means after bedtime. The house is all quiet, and we know we will be able to focus without munchkin interruptions. If you are a single parent, you may want to share your plans with a close friend or relative. This will allow you to be accountable and have your own loved one cheering you on. If your kids are a little older, then consider including them in the planning. Planning out the budgeting and sticking to it will be a great bonding experience. This will also teach your kids how to budget their own money, setting them up for financial success in the future.

How to Prevent Financial Pitfalls

Even the best-laid-out plan can experience a moment of regression when things happen that throw your plan a curveball. The following are a few common pitfalls that happen to people and some simple solutions to help you along the way.

Do Not Impulse Buy

When you see something you hadn't planned to buy and don't actually need, don't purchase it on the spot. Go home and think it over. If you decide it is something you would like to have, then add it to your budget and save for it. If the item is really worth it, you will save for it. If you don't want to take the time to save for it, then you probably don't really need it. Just because something is on sale does *not* mean you need to buy it. It is not a good deal if you don't really need it.

Avoid Charging It

The whole credit card debate is one that financial experts are constantly talking about. The debate is on whether they are beneficial or not. I have dedicated a whole chapter to credit cards, but I do have one thing to say here: If you have to purchase something on a credit card because you do not have the cash for it, more than likely you do not need that item. Credit cards are for emergencies. Never forget that.

> *"Save on electricity [and] gas and increase the lifespan of your clothes by hanging them out to dry. In the dry winter months, this can help humidify the air, keeping it comfortable at lower temperatures. Your wallet will thank you!"*
>
> *—Meghan P. (Oak Harbor, WA)*

Don't Give in to Peer Pressure

Peer pressure is real, and we still feel it as adults. If your friends, family, and close colleagues tend to be reckless regarding their finances, stay away. Just like that nasty cold someone shared with you, you can catch some contagiously bad spending habits as well. You don't want to get caught trying to keep up with someone who either has more money than you do or who is spending money he or she doesn't have. Don't get pulled into that trap. If you do, it's your own fault. Make your own decisions. Be in control of your situation, and be a leader not a follower.

Don't Compare Yourself to Others

You and your family have different circumstances than others. Remember that everyone has different income levels and is in different seasons of life. If you work to understand your finances, have control of your spending, and are saving the appropriate amount, then you are on the right track. Don't try to determine if your net worth is more or less than your peers'. Just be sure it is growing at the right pace for you. Getting sidetracked by the problems or good fortunes of others can be a distraction that needs to be avoided. It will only leave you feeling bad, and that is not what this frugal journey is about. It is about gaining confidence and knowing that you can do hard things and flourish.

Use Technology to Stay on Top of Your Finances

We live in a world that is constantly becoming more technologically advanced. For some of us who are tech savvy, this is no big deal. We have our smart phones and know how to maneuver any website put in front of

> "We are huge bookworms in our family. We have a Kindle that someone gave us, and we are always downloading free books, or we take movies, books, and video games to a local bookstore for trade-in credit. We have [earned] up to seventy dollars in credit before. It saves us so much money on our reading."
>
> —Elizabeth H. (Winston-Salem, NC)

us. My generation is a generation that has grown up with computers. We learned them in school, playing *Oregon Trail* and *Where in The World is Carmen San Diego?* We have seen cell phones go from Zach Morris's brick phone to flat, colorful touch screens.

If you are not naturally tech savvy, do not let that discourage you. You are not alone. Many cities offer free computers classes through local recreation centers, senior centers, and libraries. Check to see what classes are being offered in your area. With so many things being paid and tracked online, learning to operate a computer is a great way to stay on top of your finances. I have worked with many families who were not tech savvy. This hurt their budgets because they were not keeping track of the way they were spending. Once they were able to get the knack of computers and online banking, they had a huge turnaround in their budgets. We have this amazing technology out there to help us. Take advantage of it. Do a bit of research and learn a new skill.

Watch for Bank Fees

We can all fall victim to bank fees if we are not careful. No one is immune. Make sure you are checking your accounts often so you can see if you are being charged by your bank. Some banks require balances to be kept within a bank account or a fee will be charged each month. For some, this will result in a five-dollar charge each month. I know that five dollars may not seem like a lot, but over the course of twelve months, those five dollars add up to sixty dollars. That is money you are just handing over to your bank. Some banks also require one automatic deposit each month to prevent fees from accumulating. Know your bank rules for the accounts that you hold so you don't fall victim. I don't know about you, but I don't want to give away my hard-earned money; I want to keep it. So be aware of the rules for your bank, and make sure you are following them.

ATM usage fees are another common and totally unnecessary bank fee. Most of these fees are charged to people who use an ATM from another bank. For example, if you primarily bank with Bank of America but use a Wells Fargo bank to withdraw money, you will be charged a fee for using an ATM that does not belong to your bank. Usually it is a two- to four-dollar fee, depending on the financial institution. Be aware of these charges. Most banks charge them, and they can add up really fast. I once worked with a lady who was not aware that every time she was getting money out of the bank, she was paying an extra two dollars for her ATM withdrawals. Over a course of six months, she had paid out over forty dollars in bank fees. This was money that she was literally giving away because she was not using an ATM that belonged to her bank.

Round up When Budgeting

When you are compiling your list of bills for your initial budget, round up. Most utility bills will fluctuate a bit. Because of this, I like to round up to the nearest dollar when I am budgeting. It is much easier to budget a bit higher and receive a lower bill, because the money is still in your account to cover it. I also think working with whole numbers is a whole lot easier. When you underestimate your bills, it becomes much harder because you do not have those extra dollars available in your account. Rounding up prevents this type of budgeting problem.

Stop Putting Things Off (Deferred Payments)

A deferred payment plan is a horrible mess to get into. I have seen many individuals who have put off today's bills to be paid tomorrow. The bills that you are deferring will not go away. They will still be waiting for you next month, along with your new bill. I recently worked with a woman who had been deferring her bills because she was not able to pay them. She had stretched her finances far beyond their limits. She kept putting bills off to pay another day in the hope that she could pick up more hours at work or get a financial bonus of some sort. These hours were not always given, and that bonus was nowhere on the horizon, so that hope did little for her. She still had past-due bills to be paid along with the current monthly bills. This pattern continued to occur, and she accrued quite a buildup of past-due notices in her mailbox. This happened in just a few short months. She was behind on so many things because she had put off today's bills to pay at a later time. Be wise, and don't do this. Pay today's bills with today's money.

Set Reasonable Financial Goals

Whether you are riding solo or have a partner in crime, you need to set reasonable financial goals. People who set reasonable financial goals can avoid a lot of life's stresses. You want to think of goals that you can realistically achieve. It may take some time and a lot of hard work, but you can do it. Channel the Little Engine That Could and chant, "I think I can. I think I can."[4] It seriously helps. I do it all the time.

Setting reasonable financial goals can also help you avoid the pitfalls of being burdened by unnecessary debt. As a family, you should plan to budget your income carefully so you do not overextend yourself in the purchase of an expensive home and furnishings. Decide now how you want to live. Whether you are just starting out or have been on the road of life for quite some time, if you want a future that doesn't have you living paycheck to paycheck or shackled to debt, then decide *now* to live in a way that will get you out of those shackles.

Choose today not to spend money on something you don't need. Choosing today means that you are taking the first step in the right direction. Remember that the first step is always the hardest, but it is the most important one.

When Hubby and I first started out on our frugal journey, we made some financial goals. We had many pillow talk conversations deciding, dreaming, and planning the kind of life we wanted. We wanted to pay off our car and eventually pay cash for a house. We knew that ultimately we wanted to be debt-free and that it would take some dedication, self-control (especially on my part), and discipline, but together we knew we could do it. These were some big goals, but they were goals that we would be able to achieve. Setting goals together was an amazing thing because it put us on the same team. This is important. Many couples argue over finances, so if you can get yourselves on the same page, you will have your own hallelujah moment, just like I had when I finally started saving. We also set goals for the way that we shopped. We decided to start buying secondhand and save the difference. We started taking control of our finances, and little by little we saw that our goals were being achieved.

We didn't have just one gab session where we made financial goals; we had many. In fact, we still have them often. We love to dream and think about what the road ahead holds for us. We don't know everything, but we know that together, hand in hand, we can get over any bump because we are a united front.

Throughout our marriage, Hubby has gotten flack from guys at work when he would call and ask if it was okay to buy something. They didn't understand why the one who was "bringing home the bacon" had to ask permission to use the money he worked hard for. Hubby always politely told them that he and his wife were a team that made financial choices together. We talk about the money we are going to spend so that we are both aware of where our money is going.

If you are an individual, make sure you think often about what your personal financial goals are. This is the same for couples and families. Talk often and communicate. The more open and vocal you are, the better off your situation will be.

Save for a Rainy Day

If you have made your budget and found that all the numbers crunch into the perfect combination, then you have some wiggle room to help prepare for your family's future. Having leftover money at the end of the month is something we all strive for. Who doesn't want a little something extra after all the bills are all paid? We're all nodding our head in agreement, right? I know I am! Although your first thought may be to run buck wild and spend it, the smart thing to do is to save it. It is enticing to see how our budgeting is working and that we are actually left with a surplus. The positive sign in the bank account just makes my heart go thump, thump—in a good sort of way. It makes all that hard work worth it. Whether it was from extra hours given at work, a birthday check from Grandma, or a utility bill that was a bit less this month, a little bit of financial wiggle room is a great blessing.

We need to think ahead. Life happens. Water heaters break, car batteries die, and children get cavities. All of those things are unexpected, and if we do not have a little something saved for a rainy day, they can wreak havoc on our budgets. I will share some more about how to budget for these things later on in chapter two, but for right now, I just want to plant that little seed in your mind so you can think about those rainy days that will ultimately come your way.

With my family's budget, we save that extra money left after a long month of frugal living. These extra dollars become quite precious because they allow us to be ahead of the game next month. That little bit left at the end of the month will add up. If you are left with $40 at the end of the month and you choose to save it over a twelve-month period, you would have saved $480. You can see where that extra money adds up over time. That is money that may help you later on.

At one point in our marriage, Hubby was between jobs. We weren't sure how long it would take him to find a new one. Many friends and family were worried about us, thinking that we were surely struggling, but we weren't struggling. We had been saving our extra money for a rainy day. When the rainy day came, we were all right. We lived off of our savings for a few months while Hubby searched for a new job.

We don't always know when a rainy day will come. You could get injured at work and be out of commission for a while. You may be fired or have your hours cut back. These are things that are out of your control and can cause great stress. Having a financial reserve will allow you and your family to live well. I'd love to tell you that rainy days are not on your horizon, but they happen to everyone. No one is immune. We will all have times in our lives when the rain will pour. When that rain starts coming, unexpected expenses will occur, so make decisions today that will help you in the future. Let's be like the wise man in that children's song. Let's build a strong foundation so the rain can't wash us away.

NOTES

1. "The Wise Man and the Foolish Man," The Church of Jesus Christ of Latter-day Saints, accessed March 18, 2015, https://www.lds.org/music/library/childrens-songbook/the-wise-man-and-the-foolish-man?lang=eng.

2. Steve Economides and Annette Economides, *America's Cheapest Family Gets You Right on the Money: Your Guide to Living Better, Spending Less, and Cashing in on Your Dreams* (New York: Crown Business, 2007), 41.

3. Gordon B. Hinckley, *Cornerstones of a Happy Home*, speech given on January 29, 1984 (Salt Lake City: The Church of Jesus Christ of Latter-day Saints, 1984), 9, https://www.lds.org/bc/content/shared/content/english/pdf/language-materials/33108_eng.pdf?lang=eng.

4. Watty Piper, *The Little Engine That Could* (New York: Grosset & Dunlap, 2012).

Chapter 2

Implementing a Budget and Making It Work for You

In my world, budgeting is taking the money my family has and saving it in specific categories. These different categories allow us to save in advance for things so that when unplanned expenses happen, we are prepared. Nothing is worse than something breaking and having no money to replace it. Things break, so if we can plan a bit for those unforeseen circumstances, we can make our lives a little bit easier. Wouldn't we all like to make things a bit easier? I know I would! This type of financial planning eliminates almost 90 percent of financial emergencies. Planning ahead for economically trying times is just something responsible people do. Are you ready to dive in? Let's get to it!

The Budget Spreadsheet: How It Works

We keep track of our finances by dividing them into multiple categories. When we first started out on our frugal journey, we only included a few categories. We mainly kept to the initial budget mentioned in chapter one. That is a great budget for beginners. As we gained steam though, we realized that by planning ahead, we could anticipate about 98 percent of our annual expenses. It is not as difficult as it sounds. With a bit of planning and organization, you can plan ahead for your family's expenses and save while you do it!

I mentioned that budgets are personalized for the people living them. That is why I love budgeting with categories. You will find that you add and eliminate categories as income changes, bills are paid off, and life continues. You're not going to have orthodontist bills for forever, and someday you *will* get the car paid for. While I'll illustrate with my own budget, know that yours will be different, but it will work just as well if you apply the principles of good budgeting.

The basis of my budgeting system is simple. It is essentially about saving predetermined amounts of money from every paycheck or source of income to cover upcoming expenses. In layman's terms, it is about thinking ahead so you are not blindsided by future bills. It is about being a step ahead in this financial game. For example, we own our house, so we do not have to pay a mortgage, but we do have to pay property taxes every three months. Instead of having an $80 bill due every three months, we spread that bill out over the three months. Each month, we save $26.67 into our property taxes account. This account is really just a division of our bank account that we keep in a spreadsheet on our computer.

My budgeting system accumulates money before it is needed, meaning that my family saves for future bills before they happen. There was a time when we didn't live this way. We would live paycheck to paycheck and would be completely knocked for a loop when the unexpected happened. We usually ended up charging those expenses, and then were left with quite a nasty pile of debt. Over time, we learned that thinking in advance put us ahead, and we were able to stay out of debt. The following list includes a few common household finance categories. You may not use all of these at first, but over time you can add categories to make your budget work for your family.

Record Every Expense

Since Hubby and I got married, we have always had one banking account. For our family, we find it to be best when we share everything. We both work hard to make our family run. We do this financially, spiritually, and physically. Neither of us contributes more than the other. We appreciate what the other contributes to the family, and we work as a team to make our family unit work. Any financial contributions we have are added to our joint checking account, and that is the money that we live off of to support our family. In the example spreadsheet, you'll see categories that might be included in an average budget. This family's combined income for this particular month was $3,698. That $3,698 was divided up into smaller chunks allotted to specific categories. For example, $1,200 was set aside for mortgage or rent and $94.00 to pay cell phone bills.

Income Source	Amount	Fixed Expenses	Amount	Difference
Income Source #1	$3,698.00	Tithing/Charitable Donations	$433	
		Mortgage/Rent	$1,200	
		Homeowners' Insurance	$42.00	
		Cable/Internet	$62.99	
		Hulu/Netflix	$27.99	
		Cell Phone	$94.00	
		Car Payment	$250.00	
		Gas (Heat)	$18.00	
		Electricity	$68.00	
		Trash	$15.00	
		Water	$52.00	
		Car Insurance	$66.20	
		Clothing	$50.00	
		Groceries	$450.00	
		Eating Out	$35.00	
		Family Night	$50.00	
		Vacations	$100.00	
		Gifts	$25.00	
		Gas (Car)	$100.00	
		Thrifting	$50.00	
		Home Repair	$50.00	
		Haircuts	$25.00	
		Medical Expenses	$50.00	
		Reserve/Savings	$213.82	
		Food Storage	$20.00	
		School Supplies	$20.00	
		Car Maintenance	$25.00	
		Toiletries/Makeup	$30.00	
		Cleaning Supplies	$25.00	
		Birthdays/Celebrations	$50.00	
Total Income:	**$3,698.00**	**Total Expenses:**	**$3,698.00**	**$0.00**

Since I do the majority of the shopping, I keep our main spreadsheet on my laptop and save all of our receipts in my purse. This is an easy way for me to stay on top of things. Both Hubby and I have debit cards. When Hubby runs errands or does a bit of shopping, he lets me know how much he spent and where so I can input the expense into our spreadsheet. All of

Ask yourself if what you are doing today is helping you get closer to where you want to be tomorrow. These are words we try to live by, so we are always reaching for those goals we set for ourselves individually and as a family.

☙

Use LED bulbs instead of incandescent ones. LED lights use less energy to produce the same amount of light as incandescent bulbs.

☙

To save on our water bill, Hubby installed low-flow shower heads. This reduces the amount of water we are using daily.

☙

To save on summer cooling, we use blackout curtains to keep that hot sun at bay.

our expenses are paid out of our joint checking. This makes keeping track of and recording expenses easy.

When we spend money, we put it into our spreadsheet. We have our budget divided not only by the bills we have to pay but also by the different categories we are saving money into. You can also download phone apps or purchase software to help you do the same thing. If you are not as technologically inclined, then keep track of your expenses in a three-ring binder.

Each category has its own section in our spreadsheet. We list what we budget for the category every month. Every time we make a purchase in that category, we deduct that amount from the money budgeted in that particular category. Our spreadsheet is an account register of each specific category. We find that being able to keep track of individual categories allows us to better prepare for future expenses.

We are specific with our categories, so we do not have a miscellaneous category or catchall. We want every single thing we spend accounted for and going toward something.

Sign up for Online Banking, and then Double Check Your Math

Hubby and I are human, which means that we can make mistakes, and we do—quite often. Forgetting to carry the two can really wreak havoc on a budget, so we like to always double check our math. Our online banking is crucial to this step. You can't manage your finances efficiently without having access to an online banking system, and most banks offer this for free. At least once a month, Hubby and I sit down and go over each expense recorded in our online bank account. We then compare this to our spreadsheet to make sure that our numbers add up. If we are off, then we recheck our math.

Making It a Habit

At the beginning of each week, I sit down and put our expenses into our spreadsheet. I go through our online banking to see what purchases we have made recently. I save all my receipts, so I know what each purchase was made for and what category it goes into. If I didn't save my receipts, then I may forget why I spent fifteen dollars at the store. With my receipts, I can see that five dollars of that money went to purchase hair dye, which comes out of our category for hair. The rest of that purchase was for school supplies, which comes out of another category. Having the receipts for reference makes inputting everything much easier.

I know this may sound like a lot of work, but once you get the hang of it, it becomes second nature. Doing this once a week means I only have to take about fifteen minutes to double check our expenses and make sure that all bills due that week have been paid. Whether you do it once a week or twice a month, make sure you do it. At the end of every month, Hubby and I review the budget for the following month. Since income can fluctuate from month to month, we like to know exactly what is coming in each month, and we adjust our budget accordingly. We make plans for the future. We try to think ahead to upcoming expenses, like the yearly checkups for the kids or the oil that needs to be changed in the car.

Thinking ahead and saving for those things enables you to have more financial freedom. You are not charging things because you do not have the cash for it. You are thinking ahead and using the money saved within those categories to cover the expenses for your family. No one is left wondering if there is enough money for everything. You know there is enough because you can see it in black and white. Over time, this pattern of smart budgeting becomes a habit that takes only minutes each week but pays huge financial dividends. Like most good habits, it feels cumbersome and time-consuming when you start. Don't give up! Within two or three months, you'll have your system running smoothly, and your monthly time investment will be minimal.

Making Your Budget Work for You

As you budget, over time you will be able to truly see what your family spends on different things. I once helped a lady who swore she only spent two hundred dollars on groceries and nothing more. Over a few months of setting a grocery budget and not being able to stay within it, she realized that her original estimation was way off. This is the awesome thing about this budgeting system: it can be changed and adjusted to meet your family's personal needs. You can adjust the amounts within your categories, giving more to one category than another. As long as your account allocations don't exceed your monthly income, you will be all set!

Other Ways to Save

Using a spreadsheet on the computer is not the only way to divide your money into categories and save. You can also use the cash envelope system. To make this work, you set aside predetermined amounts of cash (from your income) and place them into envelopes. Leave enough in your bank account to cover all the fixed expenses, such as mortgage or rent, utilities, car payments, and so on. Once you get your predetermined cash from the bank, you place it into labeled envelopes representing the various categories of your budget. You then can use only whatever money is in that envelope. For example, if you took out four hundred dollars for groceries, that money would go into your "grocery" envelope and be used only for groceries.

I like this system because it brings to realization the connection between money and the material things you buy. When we use cash, we tend to think more about what we are spending it on, and we literally see that the envelope is getting thinner. That's why this technique is great for beginners. When you run out of cash in any particular envelope, the spending stops. You cannot spend money you don't have. Using cash really drives home a visual and emotional understanding for how a budget has to work in order to be successful.

I only use the cash system for purchasing groceries. For all of our other categories, I like knowing our money is secure at the bank. I am too much of a worrier, so carrying limited amounts of cash helps me sleep better at night. I use spreadsheets to accomplish the same thing many people use the envelope system for.

Build a Reserve

Gradually build a financial reserve and use it for emergencies only. If you save a little money regularly, you will be surprised how much accumulates over time. Determine beforehand a specific amount that you would like to set aside for savings. It does not need to be a large amount. As long as you are consistent with setting that money aside, it will add up quickly. Avoid giving in to the temptation to spend your savings on unnecessary things. If you discipline yourself, you will be prepared for any financial trial that comes your way. Once you have a financial reserve set aside for emergencies, you can continue to save for future needs like education, retirement, and other necessities.

Pay Tithing

For myself and my family, it is important that we pay tithing. Our tithing goes to The Church of Jesus Christ of Latter-day Saints and is used to help finance local and international Church programs and humanitarian efforts. We "tithe" a portion of our income, as mentioned in the Bible, as a way to give back to our loving Father in Heaven. Your version of tithing may be to set aside a sum for a charitable organization you admire or any kind of contribution to the improvement or blessing of others. If you do not pay tithing, no worries. You can skip this section. For those of you who do, I wanted to show you how we pay tithing and make it easier on ourselves.

There was a time when paying tithing was quite a struggle for me. I had read the scriptures and heard the talks about how paying an honest tithe would bring great blessings. Although I knew and believed this to be true, I would often wait till the end of the month to pay it, only to realize that I had already spent it. This cycle continued for quite a long time. Finally I confided in that sweet hubby of mine. I told him how I was having trouble paying our tithing. That wonderfully patient man listened and then came up with a great idea. He said that we should no longer pay tithing with a check. Too often, I would write the check, only to leave it on our desk and forget to hand it in. Because of this, Hubby and

I decided to start paying in cash. At the beginning of each pay period, we take out the cash to cover tithing. By pulling out the cash before we do anything else, we know that the money has already been removed from our account. The rest left in our account from that pay period is what we have to work with. Paying in cash was a game changer for us. Since we began paying in cash, we no longer struggle with being able to keep up.

For our family, paying tithing has blessed us by leaps and bounds. I know that our Father in Heaven is aware of our needs. When we serve Him and choose to follow Him, He provides for us. I have seen Him do great things in my life. I am always thankful for the opportunity I have to serve and give glory to Him.

We have found that this part of our financial plan actually helps us to *succeed* with our budget rather than making it harder to stretch the money. It's a paradox you'll find often. If you don't believe me, find someone else who tithes their income, and ask them why they do it.

Just Say No to Overdraft Fees

If you have bills that are scheduled to come out of your bank account, make sure you have enough money to cover them. Once your bank account has suffered a negative balance due to anything other than a system error, financial institutions will penalize you with a charge. This charge is known as an overdraft fee. Overdraft fees are the bank's way of assessing a fine when you try to use money you don't have, whether you did it knowingly or not. These fees will wreak havoc on your budget, but if you are managing your money wisely, they can be completely eliminated.

I like to think of overdrafts as giving your money away while getting nothing in return. It is not like donating money to a great cause. Instead, it's a source of financial embarrassment—a clue that you are not in control—and this causes a mix of shame, embarrassment, and absolute frustration. Banks already have enough money. We do not need to go handing them more because we weren't paying attention and being smart with our money. Here's a visual that might help you. The next time you incur an overdraft fee, take a twenty-dollar bill out of your wallet and throw it in the trash. No one in their right mind would throw twenty dollars in the trash, but this one twenty-dollar lesson may help you or your spouse visualize just how dumb it is to incur an overdraft fee. Since I know I am not the only mama out there who has ever had an overdraft fee, I figured I would share a few pearls of wisdom that have helped me along the way. I have put together a few tried-and-true steps to keep you out of the overdraft club, because that is a club that no one wants to be a part of.

Steps to Avoid Overdraft Fees

1.   *Do not rely on your "available balance."* Many banks offer you an "available balance." So nice of them, right? Well, yes and no. It does let you know what is currently in your account, but it does not take into consideration any outstanding charges scheduled to post to your account that day. It also does not reflect transactions that occurred at the end of the business day. When some transactions are run as credit, it will take longer for them to post to your account, which can trigger overdraft fees if you are spending money based on the idea that since your "available balance" is two hundred dollars, you have two hundred dollars available to spend.

2.   *Keep your checkbook balanced.* Now, I am aware we live in a digital age and everything is being done on computers. I get it. I primarily do our banking online, but that doesn't mean I don't "balance my checkbook." My method is a bit different than my grandma's method, however. I use my handy spreadsheet to be certain that my expenses match what the bank says I spent. Keeping a checkbook balanced means that all bills and expenses are accounted for. If you are having trouble with overdraft fees, you may be cutting it too close where your checkbook or spreadsheet is concerned.

3.   *Try a little discipline.* If you've set up your budget and your system for tracking expenses, don't undermine it by trying to cheat yourself. Don't go to the ATM, don't use the credit card, don't write a check. Discipline yourself to stick to the budget. Once you have used the allotted amount, don't spend more. Do not base your spending off of what is left in the account, but base it rather by what you have on your spreadsheet. This will help you to not overspend in your various categories.

4.   *Create a cushion.* This is something my parents have always supported. My dad learned early on that having a financial buffer can be quite a blessing. This cushion, which will be different for everyone, is be a life-saver when overspending happens. Decide as a family what you want your cushion to be. It could be $100 or $1,000. It is up to you and what you can realistically keep in your account. Once you decide on a cushion

number, stick to it. Pretend that once you hit that number you have run out of money. If your account has a minimum balance to avoid monthly fees, keep that amount "hidden" in your account and pretend it isn't there. Another good idea is to subtract it out of your checkbook or spreadsheet so that the balance you see is what you have to work with.

5. *Research overdraft protection.* If you have trouble keeping track of your expenses in relation to your actual balance, you may want to look into an overdraft protection program in which your main account is linked to a secondary account (like your savings account). If your main account is overdrawn, money can be pulled from the secondary account, and you don't get slapped with an overdraft fee. Just make sure that you don't use this as a security blanket. Overspending is no good whether you have the protection or not, so keep that in mind when budgeting.

I love teaching about budgeting and finances. I remember being that girl—the girl who didn't know how to make the numbers crunch together. I remember being that girl who didn't really have a clue when it came to running a household financially. It takes practice, and there are lots of us who had to learn the process slowly. Don't be embarrassed because no one has ever taught you. You've taken control by picking up this book.

Use It or Lose It

Making a budget and using a budget are two totally different things. We can come up with the best budget possible, but if it doesn't work for us or we choose not to follow it, then no good will come out of it.

I recently worked with a woman who was in a serious amount of debt. She had some problems with shopping and had created quite a hole of debt for herself. She wasn't sure what to do. She no longer had the funds to cover her debts, and things were starting to go to collections. To say she was in a pickle was an understatement. We spent a few days reviewing her finances, and we came up with a plan. We wrote it all down and made sure that what we came up with would work for her. Would she have to make some changes? Absolutely. She could no longer shop till she dropped. After much planning, she was left on her own to either sink or swim. She had all the tools: she just needed to use them. She was given that life preserver and needed to decide if she was going to wear it or not.

After a few weeks, I checked in with this lady, but the news was not good. After our initial talk, she hadn't glanced at her budget once. She had gone back to old habits and had dug herself into an even bigger hole. She had a budget, but because she never followed it, it did her little good. A budget is not something to make, look at once, and then go on your way. It should be your lifeline each day. You should cling to that thing so you can get out of the sea of debt you are in.

Living a budgeted life is kind of like building a house. An architect draws up plans for a house. He or she looks at the space it will fit in and finds a way to make the house work for the lot size it will be built on. Then the builders move in and begin to construct the architect's vision. They take measurements and constantly refer back to the plans so they know they are building it accordingly. The house is not finished overnight. It takes time. They may have a few drawbacks, and a need to reassess things may arise, but the builders keep moving forward with the building. Eventually, a beautiful house stands where there once was an empty lot.

A budget works the same way. We become like an architect, planning our budget based off the income we currently have. We work with a certain amount of money just like an architect works within a certain lot size. Over time, our budgeting ability grows and becomes stronger as we become more experienced with our frugal living. At first, you may not be able to save for that college fund for your children, but over time you will get to the point that you can. Baby steps. Eventually you will be able to look back at your finances and be like that proud architect seeing his or her vision come to life in that fully built, gorgeous house. It will take time, but it can be achieved. We have to learn to change our habits from being just okay to good to better to best. It is a process, but it is absolutely attainable.

You Can Do Hard Things

Never forget that no matter how hard it may seem at first, you can do this! You *can* do hard things. Don't allow the doubts to seep in. Don't become dormant in your ability to move forward with your life and finances. Just like my favorite scripture in Philippians 4:13, "I can do all things through Christ which strengtheneth me." Starting to live a new way can and will be challenging. You're rewiring your brain every day. You are changing old habits and making new, healthy ones. This frugal journey you are going on is one that will teach you so much.

I have seen firsthand how people have chosen to change and how it has made their lives better. I was recently working with a sweet mother of five whom I will call Annie. Annie is a hardworking single mother, trying to provide for her family. She works multiple jobs to keep up with all the bills that come her way. Recently, she had hit a wall. She felt she was at her wit's end. She didn't believe that life had to be this hard, but she didn't see any other way to live it. She had been praying for some solution to help get her life organized and back on track financially. The Lord had heard her reverent prayers. A few days after she sent up that prayer, I ran into Annie at a Church activity. I could tell from her tired eyes that she was exhausted. Because of all of her responsibilities, life had become something she endured rather than something she enjoyed. After running around from one job to the next, she would come home and try to make sense of the bills that would be waiting in the mailbox. She said that she felt stagnant. She couldn't go back and change the unwise financial decisions she had made, but she couldn't move forward either. Her poor financial choices had caused her to have little to no financial freedom. As we get behind on bills and go into debt, we begin to have fewer and fewer choices. We are literally put into financial bondage, with debt as our master. We no longer have the freedom to choose with our money. We must constantly pay off the debt collectors instead of getting ahead. This is what had happened to Annie. She had come to believe that she would be stuck with her debts forever, always drowning and never really able to come up for air.

My heart ached for this poor woman. I remember all too well being that girl who thought that this was how life was supposed to be. I didn't like being that girl who felt like she had no control over her life. I shared this with Annie. I wanted her to know that I *knew* where she was coming from. I knew how hard life can be and how sometimes we can get thrown quite a few nasty curveballs. I gave her a big hug and told her that we would find a way to make things better. She could become an independent woman and stand up for herself financially to support her family. That same night, we sat down and talked about her finances. She laid it all out. She shared the truth about her debts, her trials, and everything in between.

That first night, it took a few hours to sift through all the bills and come up with a workable budget. We modeled her initial budget off of the one that is shown on page 23. That first night was long and exhausting, but she had done it. She had made a budget. What a victory that was to celebrate! We did our own little happy dance in the middle of her kitchen that night. She wasn't out of debt, and she still had loads of bills to pay, but now she had a plan—a plan that was realistic and could work for her and her family.

Over time, Annie figured out how to budget. It wasn't something that was learned or fixed overnight. As each month passed, she saw that light at the end of the tunnel become brighter and brighter. She was able to enjoy time with her children more because her thoughts were no longer consumed with, "How am I going to pay these bills?" Because she had made a budget and was working hard, she knew that her bills would get paid. Each week, I would visit her, and we would talk over what she had done that week and the goals she had reached. Little by little, her debt lessened. Little by little, she smiled more. I could see the weight that had been on her shoulders start to be lifted. If you have ever felt like this, bogged down by your finances, know that not all hope is lost.

Creating and following a budget *is* for everyone. No matter your income level or season of life, a budget will help you take the money you receive each month and not only pay all your bills but also get you out of debt and plan for fun things in the future. Gordon B. Hinckley once said, "Set your houses in order. If you have paid your debts, if you have a reserve, even though it be small, then should storms howl about your head, you will have shelter for your wives and children and peace in your hearts."[1] We must put our houses in order and make them strong. Be smart in your planning and always know you can do this. You can truly make the impossible *possible*!

NOTES

1. Gordon B. Hinckley, "To the Boys and to the Men," October 1998, https://www.lds.org/general-conference/1998/10/ to-the-boys-and-to-the-men?lang=eng.

Chapter 3

How to Cut Your Grocery Budget in Half

In 2012, things were financially tight for my family. My husband had gotten out of the army at about the same time that economic crisis hit the country. The unemployment rate in our state skyrocketed, and he could not find a job, despite searching for months. No one was hiring. We were in quite a pickle. We had tightened our belts, but we were literally on the last belt loop with nowhere else to go. Hubby decided to enroll in college, taking advantage of the GI Bill that he was able to use because of his time in the military. While he went to college, I was in charge of feeding my family on a very small income. This is where my "Cut Your Grocery Bill in Half" post was born on my blog. It soon became one of my most popular blog posts. Every month, people are brought to my blog because of it. (Thank you, Pinterest!) Across the nation, people want to know how to cut costs and save their families money. The grocery bill is one of the only expenses you control completely. With careful planning and a little perseverance, you can shrink that expense.

I want you to feel stocked with as many money-saving tools as you can get when you enter that grocery store. The more prepared you are, the better off your grocery budget will be. Not every tip will work for your family. It will depend on where you live, your family's income, and what specifically works for you. Just like with everything in this book, pull out the ideas that you can try right now. Start with one or two things. This will help you get started in this money-saving journey. Then as you master each trick, you can try something new.

Set a Budget and Pay Cash

When you are starting out on your budgeting journey, the grocery bill is one thing you have absolute control over. With your grocery bill, you are not locked into a contract like you are with cell phone or rental agreements. You are not stuck with a monthly rate like you are with the Internet and cable or a fixed percentage rate like you are with a mortgage. These fixed expenses can't be negotiated once you've incurred them. Once you have a car payment, you can't change the amount without selling the car or paying off the debt. A grocery bill is different, and that's why it's the most important expense to learn to control.

Just like anything else on this financial journey, you must start with a plan. There was a time when I would go grocery shopping every single week. I would have no list or no budget, and I would go shopping hungry. I had made three of the worst mistakes for grocery shopping. If you don't have a plan, then you don't know what to buy. If you don't have a budget, then you don't know how much you can spend. And if you go hungry, you are just begging to have a cart full of guilty-pleasure foods. Mine are REESE'S Peanut Butter Cups, diet cream soda, and canned tropical fruit. You can't make a week's worth of meals out of those ingredients, but you can wreck your budget by purchasing them when you don't need them and can't afford them.

Because you made your household budget in chapters one and two, you should have established what a reasonable grocery budget is for your family. Decide how much you will spend each month and stick to it. You may find that some months you are able to spend more than others, and that is okay. Incomes can fluctuate a bit, so being able to decrease or increase your budget accordingly will allow you to continue to stay on track.

If you are unsure of what to budget for groceries, go back and look through old receipts or check your online banking to see how much you have been spending on groceries. Look at the number and decide if it is a realistic number, or ask yourself if maybe you've been spending too much on groceries in the past. For most, the latter will be the case. When I first decided to cut my grocery bill, it was because I had added up all my purchases in a month and found that I was spending close to $800 on groceries for my family of four! I couldn't believe it. How could my family of four be spending that much on groceries? I was in complete shock. I hadn't realized how all my little trips into the grocery store for those few items were adding up. I knew I could slash that number in half. I made the goal of spending half of what we usually spent on groceries. I gave myself a budget of $400 and said a prayer. That first grocery trip was quite an experience. I had never gone through with a set amount. I used my calculator as I went through the aisles. When you go through with a calculator, it is amazing the change that takes place. You are more aware of how much each item is adding up. You suddenly weigh the options a bit more with name brand versus generic. You think twice about adding all that candy into the cart just because it looks good. It makes you more conscious of what you are tossing in.

After you set your budget and decide what is a reasonable amount for you to spend on groceries, it is time to talk about the best way to pay for groceries. I know many credit card lovers are going to disagree with me on this one, but hear me out. At the beginning of each month or pay period, get out the set amount that you have budgeted for groceries in cash. Keep this cash in an envelope. This envelope holds all your precious dollars to buy food for your family this month. Using cash will encourage you to stay within your set budget. If you leave that credit card and debit card at home, then you only have what is in the envelope to shop with. This will make you more conscious of what you are placing in the cart. You will go through the store, logging each item into your calculator so there are no surprises at check out. Using cash will save you monthly. Going over budget by five dollars each month may not seem like a lot, but over a space of twelve months, you would have spent an extra sixty dollars. It really adds up in the end, so pay in cash. Your budget will thank you for it.

> *Make produce last all month long by eating things in order.*
>
> *First: Bananas, berries, cherries, kiwis, avocado, spinach, lettuce, grapes.*
>
> *Second: tomatoes, mango, peaches, pears, melon, apricots, zucchini.*
>
> *Third: cucumbers, pineapple, pomegranates.*
>
> *Last: carrots, potatoes, celery, apples, grapefruit, and oranges.*
>
>
>
> *No need to worry about busting the plastic on your milk jug when freezing. Gallon milk jugs are made with an indentation on the side. This is to allow for expansion.*

Shop Less Often

I am a firm believer that the less time you spend in the grocery store, or any store for that matter, the less money you will spend. Think about the last time you just went into the store for a few items. Did you buy only those few items you were in need of, or did you spend a bit more? Did you impulse buy because of the lovely endcap display of goodies or because that deal was just too good to resist? It happens. Shopping less often takes away the temptation to do this. I go to the grocery store once a month. (I know what you are thinking about the state of the milk in my refrigerator, but hear me out.) At the beginning of each month, I gear up by taking stock of what I have. I make a menu plan, and I then go shopping with my cash in hand. Going once a month has allowed my family to save dramatically over the years. It also frees up a lot more time throughout the month, because I am not constantly planning a grocery trip. That means more time for munchkin tea parties and snuggles. Whether you go weekly, biweekly, or monthly, see how far you can stretch out your grocery trips. If you are a three-times-a-week shopper, try to go only once this week. Start small. I didn't start out going once a month; I worked up to it with weekly trips. Once I felt like my feet were firmly planted in this "shopping on a budget" thing, I moved to every two weeks. Over time, I was able to start shopping once a month. Find what works for you. You will be amazed at the savings! As long as you are setting a budget and sticking to it, you will save your family money.

> *"Plan multiple meals that use the same ingredient, especially buns and tortillas, so nothing goes to waste."*
>
> —Ashley R. (Centennial, CO)

Keep a Running List

Just like anything in life, if you are going to get something done, you need to have a plan. Grocery shopping is no different. There was a time in my life when I didn't make a grocery list. I would go to the store, toss things into my cart, and hope for the best. I ended up having little to work with when dinnertime came around. Going without a plan didn't work for me. I was spending far too much money, and I was buying things I thought I was out of only to come home and see three of that item in my cabinet.

Over time, I learned that if I was going to save my family money, I had to create a list. On the side of my fridge, you will find a sheet of notebook paper. It is nothing fancy. Although it is plain, it serves its purpose quite well. Throughout the month, I jot down items that we are running low on or are completely out of. Writing things down as we use them helps me to remember what things need to be replaced in our pantry. I have a good memory, but let's be realistic. Life is hectic. A lot of the time, the last thing I am thinking about is the soy sauce we ran out of last month. Writing it down once that bottle is finished or starts to get low helps me. I am all about making this frugal living thing a bit easier for myself. Having a list is also great for the other members of my family. Having the list right there on the fridge allows them to write things down when those things are used up. Just be careful with the little ones. Sometimes my kids like to get creative on what they think we have run out of. Sometimes I find ice cream and candy bars on our list. Oh, those little optimistic monkeys. They think they're downright adorable.

When a new month starts and I am ready to start my meal planning and grocery shopping prep, this list gives me a starting point that does wonders for my sanity because I don't come home without that jar of mayo I really needed for tomorrow's lunches.

Shop the Ads

Each week, grocery stores send out ads telling you what items they have on sale. Don't toss these in the trash! They are crucial for your grocery planning.

1. Make a menu plan. Knowing in advance what you plan to serve simplifies the process of planning what to buy.

2. I go through each ad and circle the things that are on sale that I would like to purchase. In my area, I have about five grocery ads to choose from. I make sure I go through each one to see what is on sale. Even if it is a store I don't normally shop at, I check the ad to look for great deals.

3. Next, I take stock of what I already have by checking the dark recesses of my pantry or freezer. There's no point in buying a bag of frozen peas on sale when I already have three bags in the freezer. I know I won't use them all before they expire, so there's no point buying more, even if they are on sale. This plan keeps me from making unnecessary purchases.

4. Next, I can start to make my grocery list, concentrating on adding items that I can purchase while they are on sale.

Check Your Pantry before Shopping

Once you have shopped the ads and created a menu plan, it is time to make that grocery list. I always start out with my running list first. This lets me know what we have used or run out of during the month. I then compare my pantry staples list to my actually pantry. If I notice we are low on stuff, I add that stuff to the list to be restocked. Next, I look at all the meals planned for the month and get together my list of ingredients. Because I keep a fairly stocked pantry, a lot of the items I need for my month's worth of meals will already be on my pantry shelves. I take my meal ingredient list and shop my pantry first, crossing stuff off as I go. If I already have it in my pantry, there is no reason for me to buy it. You always want to use what you have first so you can limit the amount of wasted food in your home.

Each month on my blog, I post a new monthly menu plan with recipes (visit www.blissfulanddomestic.com). I always encourage my readers to make their grocery list based off of that month's recipes. Once the list is made, I encourage them to go to their pantry or food storage and see what they already have in stock. It's amazing how half the shopping can be done before you even leave your home!

Keep Pantry Staples Stocked

Before each shopping trip, I check my pantry not only for what I need to make all my meals for the month but also for my pantry staples. As long as I keep my pantry staples in stock, I can make any recipe in my arsenal of cookbooks. I don't like to use ingredients that can't roll over into three or more recipes. I feel like every single item I purchase and stock up on must earn its place on my pantry self. I am a busy mama with only so much shelf space. If I am going to keep something stocked in my pantry, I want to make sure it is worth it.

Pantry Storage Space for Those without a Pantry

Part of the key to decreasing your food budget is making larger purchases when things are on sale and storing them for future use. This food storage is critical to lowering your grocery budget. I keep our pantry food and supplies stocked throughout the house. I have had to get creative with food storage because I do not have a large kitchen with tons of space. I have taken a top shelf in each of the kid's closets, where little hands can't get to it. I also store toilet paper under the boy's bed (that is one thing you never want to run out of), and I have a shelving rack next to my washer for more food. Making use of this space allows me to keep most of my pantry staples on hand. If you do not have a lot of space for storing food, get creative. As long as your food is unopened, you will not get bugs. As you look at this list, you'll notice that items from the list sometimes go on sale. That is the time to stock up so that you will have it when you need it, without paying full price.

Food Storage Pantry Staples List

My pantry list may include things your family uses, and it may include stuff that you don't. Use my list as a starting point and go from there.

Grains

Chia seeds
Cornmeal
Cream of wheat cereal
Flaxseed
Ground bran
Long-grain brown rice
Nutritional yeast
Pearled barley
Popcorn
Quick-cooking oats
Wheat berries
Wheat germ
White flour
Whole-wheat flour

Baking Supplies

Apple pie filling
Baking powder
Baking soda
Baking chocolate
Buttermilk powder
Cherry pie filling

Chocolate chips
Cocoa powder
Cornstarch
Cream of tartar
Kosher salt
Salt
Shortening
Vanilla
Yeast

Dairy

Evaporated milk
Powdered milk
Sweetened condensed milk

Sugars

Brown sugar
Corn syrup
Honey
Maple syrup
Molasses
Powdered sugar
White sugar

Oils

Coconut oil
Margarine or butter (store in freezer or fridge)
Olive oil
Sesame oil
Vegetable or canola oil

Juice

Apple juice
Grape juice
Lemon juice
Lime juice

Canned Foods

Applesauce

Cheese soup
Corn
Cranberry sauce
Cream of chicken soup
Cream of mushroom soup
Enchilada sauce
Gravy
Green beans
Green chiles
Mandarin oranges
Mushrooms
Nacho cheese soup
Peaches
Pears
Pickles
Pineapple
Salsa
Stewed tomatoes
Sweet green peas
Tomato sauce
Tomato soup

Pasta

Angel hair or spaghetti
Egg noodles
Lasagna noodles
Macaroni noodles
Manicotti noodles
Penne noodles
Rotini noodles
Shell noodles
Spiral noodles

Dried Fruits and Vegetables

Apples
Apricots
Carrots
Cranberries
Onions
Potato flakes
Raisins

Nuts

Almonds
Cashews
Hazelnuts
Peanuts
Pecans
Sunflower seeds
Walnuts

Beans

Black beans
Black-eyed peas
Chickpeas
Kidney beans
Lentils
Lima beans
Navy beans
Pinto beans

Vinegar

Apple cider vinegar
Balsamic vinegar
Distilled white vinegar
Red wine vinegar
Rice vinegar

Condiments

Apricot jelly
BBQ Sauce
Grape jelly
Hot sauce
Jalapeño jelly
Ketchup
Mayonnaise
Mustard
Peach jam
Peanut butter
Soy sauce
Strawberry jelly
Teriyaki sauce

Spices

Allspice, ground
Anise
Basil
Black pepper
Chicken bouillon, powdered
Cilantro leaves
Cinnamon
Curry powder
Dill
Garlic
Ginger
Lemon pepper
Marjoram
Mustard, dry
Nutmeg
Onion powder
Oregano
Paprika
Parsley
Pumpkin pie spice
Red chili pepper flakes
Rosemary, ground
Sage, rubbed
Seasoning salt
Spaghetti seasoning
Taco seasoning

Fun Things to Have

Cake or brownie mix
Chips
Chocolate bars
Crackers
Granola
Hot chocolate
Instant pudding or jello mix
M&M'S
Nutella
Pudding cups

My list of pantry staples are the items I like to always have on hand at all times. We use these items often, and I have learned how to calculate how much my family will use over the course of a few months. For example, I know my husband will go through four jars of spicy pickles each month. He is a pickle fanatic! Because I know how much he uses them on a monthly basis, I can stock up when these go on sale. I try to have about three months' worth of pickles on our pantry shelf. This helps for the months when pickles are not on sale or I am not able to include them in our budget.

Keeping a stocked pantry allows me to buy things only when they are at rock-bottom prices. We have also had times when our income was a bit less than normal. When those leaner months happened, we were able to eat from our food storage and not spend as much on groceries. I like to think of food storage as our food security. It is a good thing to have.

Go Homemade

Over the years, I have learned that the more we can make at home, the better off our grocery budget will be. In our home, we try to make as much from scratch as possible. From bread to pasta, to sauce, we try to go homemade if we can. With food prices escalating and preservatives ever increasing, it is nice to make pasta sauce and be able to name every single thing in it.

Using a bread machine helps us have homemade bread each week. Our family can go through about three loaves of bread a week. What can I say? Those redheads like their cinnamon toast, and so does their mom. If I were to buy that bread from the store, I would be paying over three dollars per loaf. Thirty-six dollars a month is a hefty fee to pay for something I can make in minutes for one-third

To cut down on grocery bills, buy less meat. Try substituting beans and wheat berries for meat in your favorite recipes. Enchiladas, spaghetti, and casseroles taste just as good with the meat omitted. Up the veggie amount for an added bonus.

Buying dried beans and cooking them in a pressure cooker is cheaper than buying the canned beans from the store!

Having tuna, hard-boiled eggs, peanut butter, and jelly in your home make for quick lunches for the family.

Looking for a frozen goodie for the kids? Try putting tubes of yogurt in the freezer. It makes for a yummy treat.

Dinner plans go awry? Try breakfast for dinner. It requires little prep work, and pancakes are yummy no matter the time of day.

Run out of eggs? No worries! You can use a quarter cup fruit or veggie puree for one egg in most recipes. You can also use one tablespoon flaxseed and three tablespoons water to replace one egg.

the cost. I also have the freedom of adding extra goodies into our bread, like wheat germ, bran, and flaxseed, which increase the nutritional value and makes the house smell heavenly! For days when the weather is hot and you don't want to heat up the house by turning on the oven to make bread from scratch, consider visiting an outlet store to get day-old bread at half its grocery store price. Always check expiration dates and make sure packages are well sealed if you purchase at an outlet store.

We have also found that canning some foods at home is quite beneficial. When you see fruits or veggies at rock-bottom prices, you can buy cases and can them for later use. Canning is nothing new. It is what all of our grandparents did. They learned that you store food for those times when food is scarce. Well, things have changed. Although food may not be scare in our country, it often costs a pretty penny. Being able to buy food at a low price and can it for later use in the year saves money.

Chapter 4

Become a Strategic Shopper

Most of us do not realize that the local grocery store offers dozens of savings strategies. We often work at a pace that makes it complicated to get to the store at all. This results in our paying more for things than we need to.

If you slow down and do a bit of planning, you can get a thrill from the intellectual challenge of finding clever ways to save your family money. Figuring out your store's savings programs and learning how to make them work for your family can be rewarding. It is a game I enjoy every time I go shopping. I feel like a mama on a mission, with savings as my endgame. I know that my planning and smart shopping is saving us money, and the amount I contribute to the family's bottom line (by not spending it) is a significant accomplishment. It makes all that hard work worth it. I do a victory dance in my kitchen every time I get home from shopping. Sometimes the kids join in, and sometimes they look at me with that "Mama's lost it again" roll of the eye. Thankfully, I don't get embarrassed too easily. In fact I kind of find joy in embarrassing my family with my dancing. (Sh . . . don't tell them!)

I like to celebrate my savings. It is hard work to gear up for grocery shopping, but what a great feeling it is when the shopping is done and you see all the money you saved your family. You are tackling the day-to-day grind of family and work life, while saving your family precious dollars as well. You rock!

Not only is it a fun game to learn how to be a strategic shopper, you will also end up with serious savings in the bank if you know what to look for when you shop. It pays to take time to learn how store policies and savings programs work in your area. This knowledge will help you get through your grocery shopping and save some money as well. Can I get a "Woot! Woot!" for saving money?

Use a Calculator

Once you have set a realistic budget to shop with each month, you need to have a way to keep track of it. The simplest method I've discovered is keeping a calculator with me as I shop. As I toss things into my cart, I input amounts into the calculator on my phone. I like to periodically jot down my running total on my grocery list in case I accidentally clear out the calculator. (I've done this a time or two, and it is not fun to start over again from the beginning).

When you are buying fruits and veggies, weigh them. Once you know the weight, figure out the approximate sales price by multiplying the weight by the cost per pound. I always round my weight up to make figuring out the price a bit easier. It is better to round up and stay within budget than it is to round down and have to start figuring out what to put back you realize you have overspent.

Priorities First

Many grocery stores have a similar layout. You will find the produce, dairy, and meat department on the outside of the store, while most of prepackaged snacks, crackers, canned goods, and baking stuff are located toward the center of the store. This is called "shopping the perimeter," and not only does it help you control your budget, but it also helps assure that your family is eating better because the fresh foods found in the perimeter of the store tend to be healthier choices. The basics of grocery shopping include vegetables, fruit, protein, and milk. These are the food necessities of life. These are the items you *need* to have to create a healthy meal plan for your family. This makes up the needs versus wants of grocery shopping. When you are shopping on a budget, you want to make sure that you are filling your cart with the basics first. You want to stretch the grocery budget as much as you can and make it work for you. If you have money left over, you can move into the inside aisles of the grocery store, but only if the budget allows it.

Pay for Food, Not Convenience

I once worked with a woman who desperately wanted to get her grocery spending under control, but she wasn't really sure how to go about doing it. She had been making a list and planning out a menu but was always going over budget. She never felt like she could purchase all the necessities she needed for her family on the amount of money they could budget. She couldn't raise the budget, so she desperately needed to figure out how to shop and stick to her plan. After discussing her financial woes, we took a look in her refrigerator. It was full of precut fruit and veggies. She hadn't realized that while buying the precut fruits and vegetables was more convenient, she was paying a dollar or more per item in exchange for the convenience. She hadn't even realized her mistake. Once she started paying for the *food* and not the *convenience*, she was able to stay within budget and not feel restricted. You save money when you buy the basic ingredients for your meals—like apples, ground beef, milk, and carrots—rather than prepared items.

Organic vs. Nonorganic

In the grocery world, there are a few hot-button topics, and one of the most trendy is the argument of organic versus nonorganic. I don't buy organic. I can't afford it. It is more expensive. If you feel passionate about wanting to eat organic foods, study the actual benefits rather than simply listening to popular media. Once you've made an educated decision, you'll also need to consider whether you can *actually* afford organic foods. If you are having a hard time sticking to your budget because of buying organics, you may not be able to afford it. Reassess what you are buying and look to see if you can continue buying those things. Some changes may have to be made. Maybe you buy organic fruits and veggies but stick to regular milk and meat. Everyone has a splurge item. You need to decide how to make it work for your budget.

Go with the Generic Brand—or at Least Give It a Try

When Hubby and I were first married, he was quite a brand snob. I grew up on generic. That was what my parents always bought, but Hubby refused. He claimed the difference between name brand and generic was too great for his delicate taste buds. He watched a few episodes of Master Chef with me and thought he was a food connoisseur. After months of buying name brand and realizing our small grocery budget would not accommodate these expensive options, I decided to change things up. If he was going to eat cereal, he would have to eat what I bought, and I was buying generic. We started trying out different generic brands. Boy, was he surprised when he realized that some generic brands tasted the same or even better than the name brands! He came to the realization that you are often just paying for that logo on the box. Go for generic when you can because it will save you money. There are some things Hubby and I have learned truly taste the same as the name brand, while others can't compare. The only way to know if you'll like a product is to try it.

When shopping for generics, make sure to look up and down the shelves of food. Most grocery stores put the name brand items at eye level. They want that to be what the consumer focuses on. Generic brands are usually on the bottom shelf or the top shelf, so keep those eyes open.

Remember that grocery stores are businesses providing a service. You are the consumer, and they are advertising to you. They want the shopping experience to be one that causes you to add more to your cart and spend all the money in your wallet and then some. Instead of falling for it, make the grocery store work for *you*. Try out the generic versions of some of your favorite foods and see for yourself. You just may find out you can start saving your family a lot more money.

Create a Price Book

To help save us money at the grocery store, we created a price book for the things we normally buy. A price book is a way to keep up with pricing, rotation, and sales at the stores I shop at most. It lists all the items I typically buy and what I pay for those items. Having a running list of what the normal price is for an item and what the lowest price I like to pay helps me save. Having a price book lets you know if you are really getting a good deal or not. For example, let's say you wanted to buy ketchup and you saw it was on sale for $1.25. Your price book will be a record that will help you know not only what the average price is for ketchup but also a typical "sale" price you can expect to pay if you are patient, buy on sale, and purchase in bulk. You will also notice a trend as you keep your price book updated. You will be able to see that certain items go on sale throughout the year, sometimes seasonally. You'll pay top dollar for canned pumpkin if you buy it in July, but in November, the price is cut by as much as a third. It's wise to stock up on a few extra cans in November.

A price book is really easy to keep updated as well. The best way to keep your price book updated is to look at your old receipts and store ads. Every week, you can take a few minutes and write down the various sale prices you see. You can also write down the pricing as you go through the grocery store. Having a price to compare at the store really helps. I use this a lot when I shop in bulk. Sometimes we think that buying in bulk is always the best deal. This is not always the case. Having a list of the rock-bottom prices I buy things at lets me know if that huge box of toilet paper is really the steal I think it is.

Mix-and-Match Sales

Mix-and-match sales are some of my favorites. You will see these types of sales frequently at your grocery store. If you buy a specific amount in one transaction, the store will give you a bulk discount or a percentage off the total. A local grocery store recently had a "buy five" mix-and-match sale. With these sales, you can either buy five of one item or a combination of different participating items. You mix and match participating items in multiples of five and save five dollars instantly at checkout. All items have the sales ad price tag on them so you know what items are included in that sale.

This sale was happening at my store during football season, so a lot of the items included in the sale were snacks. I decided to take advantage of that and stock up my pantry with some snacking essentials. Yes, crackers are an essential in our house—one of those "splurge" items we talked about before. Those little munchkins gobble them up, and Hubby and I can put a few away too! The store offered Wheat Thins for $1.88. They were normally $2.88, but if you bought a combination of five participating items, you received one dollar off all five items. I ended up buying 2 boxes of graham crackers for $1.99 (normally $2.99) and three boxes of Wheat Thins for $1.88. By grouping my items together and mixing and matching, I was able to save money on items we usually buy. Word to the wise: don't get overzealous in your stocking up. Make sure you are only stocking up on what your family can realistically eat before the food expires. If the food gets wasted, then it was money that was ill-used.

Ten-for-Ten-Dollars Sales

These sales are advertised where you buy a minimum number of items to pay the lower price. Many stores promote a sale price in terms of multiple items being purchased, such as 10 for $10. This seems to suggest that you, the shopper, must purchase all ten items to get the sale price. For most grocery stores, this is not true. For example, the Kroger retail chain operates several grocery stores that may go by more than a dozen different names depending on your geographic location. These include Fred Meyer, Dillons, Smith's, and many more. But the sales are similar in all of the stores in the chain at any given time. At my local Smith's, these buy-ten-for-ten-dollars items are actually priced individually, meaning you do not have to buy all ten to receive the sale price. When you see these sales at your local grocery store, ask what the store policies are. Why spend extra if you don't have to?

Know your store's policies so you can get the biggest bang for your buck. If your store does require a minimum purchase, like in the mix-and-match sale, you will see a notation on the store's ad. This should tell you what is required of that sale. Don't see a notation? Ask a store manager to make sure before you go shopping. It never hurts to ask. It is better to find out ahead of time than to get to the checkout and be surprised.

Buy One, Get One Free

These sales can be a bit tricky, so don't be fooled! At first glance, it may seem like you are getting a real steal. It is only when we take a second look that we see through the marketing. You want to be careful so you don't overspend for your items. When I see a sale like this, I like to do my math to ensure I am getting the best deal possible. Let's say cereal was priced at $4.99 per box and it was a buy-one-get-one-free scenario. I take my $4.99 and divide it by the two boxes of cereal. My math tells me that each box of cereal will cost me $2.49. I then look at my price book to see if I am getting a good deal or not. In this case, $2.49 per cereal box is a little bit more than I typically pay. Having a price book also helps me in figuring out that, in this case, the deal isn't really as good as the marketers want me to think it is.

A lot of times, the grocery store will raise the price on the item to make up for the free item you are getting. Because of this, doing your math will really help.

Price Matching

Does your store match competitor's prices? Many stores have a specific price-match policy. You can usually find these online. It is always a good idea to review these before attempting to price match so you understand clearly what your store's policies are. Most stores that price match are willing to match another store's advertised prices, if you can document the sale using the store's printed circular or online ad. If you are using an online ad, simply print that item's page from the website or show the ad via a smart phone. This is a simple method that only takes a little time but can save you hundreds on your grocery budget! Not only will you pay less for your favorite items, but you'll also save the gas you would have burned traveling to multiple grocery stores to buy what was on sale.

When I get ready to price match, I like to be organized. This saves me time and keeps me from holding up the line behind me at the grocery store. I write down each store on a sheet of paper, followed by the items I want to price match. This lets me know what I am going to buy and saves time at the register as well. As each item comes up on the conveyor belt, I tell the cashier I am price matching that item. I then look at my list, find the advertised price to give to the cashier, and know immediately what competitor's ad circular I need to show as proof of the sale.

When price matching, it is best to go at a time when your store is not too busy. Going at five o'clock—when many people are getting off of work and trying to squeeze in a quick shopping trip—is not the best time. I like

Arrange your grocery list according to the store layout. This will save you time and prevent the need for backtracking.

By cutting paper towels out of our grocery budget, we were able to save $15 a month. Over a year, that adds up to $180 in savings! Use rags or cut up shirts to wipe up spills.

To save on buying plastic food storage bags, I reuse them. If they didn't hold raw meat, I rinse them out with soap and water and place them on a rack to dry. This is just another way to save that planet of ours and some money too.

to go in the morning or late evening. These are times when stores are not as crowded, making price matching a better experience for everyone. I am a happier camper because I am not getting stink-eyed glares from those around me. The cashier is also happier because the store is not so hectic. It is a win-win for everyone.

Don't forget that kindness goes a long way. I have noticed that the nicer I am, the nicer the cashier will be. Remember that he or she is human and makes mistakes. If a mistake is made (like an item being rung up twice or a price marked wrong), do not chastise the cashier. We all make mistakes. Politely ask about the mistake so it can be corrected. Don't forget to smile. People are more likely to be helpful when they know others are being kind. I think this goes for life in general. You attract more bees with honey than vinegar.

Pay Attention at the Checkout

You've planned out your grocery trip from beginning to end. You meal planned, wrote down a grocery list, shopped the ads, went through with a calculator, and now your shopping is almost done. All that is left is the checkout. I know you're tired from all that planning. Your feet may be hurting from walking down each and every aisle in the store, but you have to stay vigilant. Don't "check out" during checkout. If you've gone through with your calculator, then you should know exactly what your grocery total will be (give or take a few dollars, depending on the sales tax in your state). Because you were smart and went through with that calculator, you will notice discrepancies in the total. If you notice that the numbers are off, don't be afraid to ask the cashier. Have him or her double check quantities of items. Make sure that all the sale prices were registered and that the correct produce codes were keyed in. When possible, pay attention to what the cashier is scanning. Staying focused is a great way to help. The cashier doesn't want to overcharge you, and you don't want to be overcharged.

If mistakes happen, remember the kindness rule. There is no need to be mean to the cashier. They are just trying to do their job. Politely ask them to go over your receipt if you notice a difference in your calculator total and the stores total. Doing all of this will save your family dollars.

I have had many occasions where I have gone to the store, gone through checkout, and then noticed that my total was a few dollars off from what I had calculated. Once the clerk and I go over the receipt, we are almost always able to find the mistake and fix it. If it was a mistake on my part, I politely thank them for going over the receipt and apologize for my mistake. If it was their fault, then I always thank them for their willingness to fix the error. Again, folks, it is all about kindness. We can save money and have a voice without being mean to those around us. Kindness is key in life, lovelies!

Coupons

Using coupons is no longer a shopping secret. There are television shows about extreme couponers and many websites teaching shoppers how to save their money by clipping coupons. Coupons can be a great way to keep grocery totals down, allowing you to get more for your money. Clipping coupons can take time, but if you follow a few simple tips, you can make coupons work for you.

I am not an extreme couponer and am most certainly not an expert. I do not go through hundreds of newspapers, looking for coupons. In my city, it would cost more to get the day-old newspapers than I would save with the coupons. In states where old newspapers are given away, going through those papers for coupons might be a great idea.

This is what has worked for my family: I clip only the coupons that come to my own mailbox. I also get coupons from friends and family who don't use theirs. I keep my coupons in an accordion-folder organizer. Each section of the accordion folder has a section of the store—from health and beauty to dairy. Keeping these coupons organized allows me to save and plan better. When store ads come out and I am planning my menu and shopping trip, I look to see if I have any coupons to go with the items I already have on my list, based on my menu plan. Combining sales, price matching, and coupons can equal amazing savings!

Newspapers are not the only place to get coupons. With a little bit of research, you'll discover that there are dozens of coupon sites, phone apps, and other tools to help you succeed. If coupon clipping is tedious and discouraging, consider enlisting one of your children and tell them you will pay them the amount that you save by using coupons they clip. This saves you time and money and gives your child some disposable income to use as they practice budgeting and shopping wisely. It's a win-win.

If you get discouraged with the time it can take to coupon, then change your mind-set. As with all of the frugal planning mentioned in this book, these are all things that take time but will help you in the long

If you have a hard time staying out of the drive-through on busy nights, stock your freezer with some frozen meals. Whether homemade or store bought, they will save you money and keep you eating healthy!

run. View coupons as cash. That is essentially what they are. The more determined you are to see them as a way to keep more money in your pocket, the more likely you will continue your clipping.

Some stores even match competitor's coupons. Many drugstore chains have their own store coupons. These come out in their weekly advertising circulars. If your grocery store accepts competitors' coupons, use them. Drugstores frequently offer coupons for health and personal care items, so it can be worth the time to check their circulars and see if your regular grocery store will honor their price. It never hurts to ask.

Some grocery stores stack coupons or double them. Check out what your store's coupon policy is so you know before you do your shopping. "Stacking" coupons is when you use a manufacturer coupon with an in-store special. This can really boost your savings. Know your store's policies before you shop so you can take advantage of whatever deals are offered. Your store may also have some great rewards programs you can take advantage of, so educate yourself about the stores where you shop.

The one thing I do want to stress is that you should never buy an item just because you have a coupon. You are not saving if it is something you don't really need. Sometimes the deal is so good, it can be rather tempting. Remember to stick to your list and use coupons only for the things you would normally buy. Also, don't buy more than you need. I love stocking up as much as the next saving diva, but clearing shelves just because you can is not cool. Make sure all the items will be used and not get wasted. If a coupon requires a certain quantity to obtain the discount, make sure you can and will use all of the items. If you don't, you run the risk of wasting money.

False: It Is Always a Good Deal

We all love getting a good deal, right? I know I sure do. When I go to the checkout and am told I saved forty dollars and only spent twenty-five dollars, I am elated. That is a great score and some great savings to boot! Although finding great sales while shopping is always a plus, it is only a great score if you need that item. Buying ten cans of sardines for twenty-five cents each sounds like a great deal, but if my family doesn't eat sardines, I am wasting my money on this deal. I am spending money on something I don't need or use. Charging or going over budget is not getting a good deal. I have worked with many couples and families in the past who have told me about their weakness for a good sale. I always remind them, "It is not a good deal if you don't need or use that item, and it isn't ever a good deal if purchasing it causes you to go over budget."

Stock up Seasonally

If you were to see what is in my shopping basket after one of my average monthly shopping hauls, you might get confused. Some months it may look like all I buy are snacks, where another month it will seem I buy only ground turkey and chicken breasts. Buying seasonally is a great way to save and build up a stockpile. Each month, grocery stores offer certain sales on items. For example, in the summer, snacks and BBQ items will be at rock-bottom prices. Most people are gearing up for holiday BBQs, which means condiments and BBQ essentials are in need. Stores take advantage of this and offer sales to entice more customers to come to their store. This is the key time to stock up. In July, I tend to stock up on chips, crackers, ketchup, relish, mayo, and mustard. These are things my family can use all year long. From June to Labor Day, these items hit all-time low prices. If it is in the budget, I try to buy not just what my family will use this month but also what we will use in the next few months. This enables me to buy things only when they are at their lowest prices.

Stockpiling food storage takes time. You build it up one can at a time. Eventually, you will be able to have a great reserve of items your family uses every day. Always make sure that your storage is full of things your family will eat. Remember the sardine tip? It applies here too.

Fill your grocery toolbox with all of these tools, and you will be able to be confident while you shop and save your family money. Remember that saving money can be fun. Think of it as a game where you are trying to save the most money you can. Challenge yourself and know that you can do this!

Chapter 5

Menu Planning
101+ Recipes

The clock is striking five, your children are running wild, your hubby is making the drive home, and you are staring into your pantry, without a clue as to what to feed your family tonight. Sound like a familiar scenario? This used to be me every night. I would find myself staring blankly into my cabinets, without a thought of what I could make for dinner. When I think back to all the time I spent standing in front of my fridge and pantry, I cringe. I would stare blankly at rows of items, without a morsel of a meal idea. It was ridiculous the time and money I wasted on food that went bad because it was not used up in time. I was so lost because I didn't have a plan. Finally, it hit me that something had to change. I needed a plan. I am a planner by heart. I make to-do lists just so I can cross stuff off. (We all do that, right?) Well, why not have a plan for what I am feeding my family too?

When I was a young mom, the five o'clock blues were a regular occurrence in my home. I had a four-year-old and an eighteen-month-old to take care of all day. I was a life-size mommy energizer bunny—on the go constantly, but before I knew it, naps had ended, and the clock told me it was five. Once again, the day had gotten away from me, and I had no clue what to feed my ravenous family. You'd think that after day in and day out experiencing the toddler whines at five, I would have gotten it together and planned something, but I didn't. I didn't have meat thawed out or something delicious in the Crock-Pot. The memo never got to me.

I thought the dreaded hour from five to six p.m. was just something all moms had to endure—like some Mommy Club initiation. Maybe I thought that if I could make it through that crazy hour of the day with

56

two hungry toddlers, I would win some kind of award. I would be able to stand on the hilltop of motherhood and say I conquered it. I would shout, "I overcame the tummy grumbles and the high-pitched whines. I am Momma, hear me roar!"

I remember when I finally learned this essential, life-altering tidbit. I was lying in bed one night, telling my hubby how I dreamed of being *Supermom*. I wanted to be that mom who always had dinner on the table, who always had a beautifully cleaned home, and who always had it together. As Hubby and I continued our pillow talk, he said something profound. He said, "Supermom doesn't exist. Women make her up in their minds." Well, my word! I couldn't believe he had just dropped that bomb on me! With my hubby's simple statement, my "Supermom" idol disappeared. She evanesced into a big cloud of white smoke. The thing was, he was right. As women, we make up these unrealistic standards for ourselves. We set goals that are often unattainable. I had envisioned a Supermom who did everything perfectly. Because that type of perfection was impossible, I never even tried, feeling I would fail from the start. I was doing myself a great disservice. Finally accepting that Supermom didn't exist was one of the best realizations I came to in my frugal journey. I realized that although I couldn't be perfect, I could be a more impeccable version of myself. I could set a small goal of planning out a week of meals. I would follow that plan until all the meals had been made. I would start off small and achieve my goal of meal planning by taking baby steps.

When babies are born, we don't feed them steak, right? They start off on their mother's milk and gradually graduate to rice cereal, mashed food, and so on. The same idea applies to us. When we are learning something new, we need to start off slow. I started out by planning one full week of meals. I wrote it on a piece of notebook paper and taped it to the fridge: spaghetti, tacos, macaroni and cheese, hot dogs, pizza, leftovers. This is the plan I followed for the entire week. I started off small so I wouldn't set myself up for disaster. If I had told myself, "Danielle, you will make everything from scratch, from the sauce to the bread," I would have gone crazy! I would have been a defeated lump of tears by the end of that first day. Start off simple so you can celebrate those small victories. Those small victories will become great successes!

What a glorious moment it was when five o'clock rolled around and I already had dinner in the oven. I did my own little jump for joy. My kids actually ate their food because they weren't filled up on snacks! I was no longer tossing bags of Goldfish crackers over my shoulder at them to buy me time while I thought of what to cook for dinner. I had finally made a plan and stuck to it. Praise everything—she can be taught! (This is what my dad would have said.) It was a pure hallelujah moment. It was absolutely glorious!

Menu Planning Helps Your Health and Your Wallet

This same idea works for those without children in the home, including those who are single and cooking for themselves. Whatever your family unit is, meal planning will save you time, money, and stress! The last one is reason enough for me. Each day, many Americans opt for a quick and cheap meal at a fast-food restaurant rather than making a meal at home. They do this without giving thought to the cost—both in terms of time and in terms of expense. That is crazy. If a family of four spends $15 on a fast-food value menu twice a week, they would spend over $120 every month. That $120 adds up quickly. In one year, that family would spend over $1,440 on fast food! Those value cheeseburgers and fries add up.

All those last-minute stops through the drive-through because you are too tired to cook or didn't plan a meal will really hurt your budget—not to mention your health. Now, I am not naive. I am like any other red-blooded American. I like my chicken nuggets and greasy cheeseburger, but eating these every week, let alone every day, is not good. Greasy burgers are high in calories and low in nutritional content. They also play havoc on your wallet.

Don't let fast food be your sanctuary—the thing you fall back on when dinner plans go awry. Eating out should be planned and something special your family does together. I will talk about this more later. When we make those unplanned trips to our local drive-through, we are spending money that was not budgeted. This unplanned spending throws our budget off because money that was allocated elsewhere has to be used to cover your trip to the drive-through. It creates a domino effect, sending your budget into the red.

Make a Plan and Stick to It

When beginning meal planning, you should start off small. Whether you are a novice or a pro, you can meal plan by following these simple tips. The first thing is to commit today is to make a meal plan and stick to it.

Start off by planning a week. Write down six meals, leaving your seventh day for leftovers. When first starting out, it is easy to give each night a theme. Monday could be Mexican night, and you could have tacos with corn on the cob. Tuesday night could be Italian themed, and you could serve spaghetti and meatballs. Give each day a theme, and the meal planning becomes a cinch.

Giving each night a type of meat you cook is also a great way to make your meal planning less daunting. Whether you use chicken, beef, or fish, themed nights are a great way to stay organized and on task. Go through your cookbooks or favorite food blogs to find meal ideas. My favorites are listed on my own blog at blissfulanddomestic.com. I am a big cookbook fan. I love finding new cookbooks at the library, which helps to keep my meal plans fresh so my family doesn't get bored with the same meals every single week. We like to change it up!

Using Leftovers

Including leftovers in your meal plan is a great way to not only save but also give yourself a night off in the kitchen. Leftovers are any part of a meal not eaten the day it was made. Saving sauces, veggies, and meats will help stretch your groceries further. Eating leftovers puts your hard-earned money back into your pockets and frees up more time to spend with that family of yours. I like to think of leftovers as getting a whole meal or part of a meal for free.

Did you know that "Americans toss about $165 billion worth of food a year" in the trash?[1] That is absurd!

"Our wasteful ways are particularly acute around the holidays." In 2012, "the National Turkey Federation said Americans were projected to buy about 736 million pounds of turkey . . . and, by one calculation, 204 million pounds

"Keep a bag of any leftover veggies in the freezer. Add to the same bag, meal after meal, . . . leftover roast or shredded chicken and enjoy a night off from cooking with your 'free' pot of soup!"

—Angela O. (Tonganoxie, KS)

"I keep a broth bag in the freezer. I put celery, onion, carrot trimmings, chicken bones, fat, skin, [and so on] into the bag as I'm cooking various meals . . . basically anything you cut off while cooking, but don't eat. I just add it all to the freezer bag. When it is filled up, I throw it into a pot with water, bay leaves, and peppercorn. I get tons of free broth this way! Freeze the broth for later use."

—Shawn L. (League City, TX)

> Have leftovers, but don't want to eat them this week? Freeze them for a quick meal later in the month.
>
> ✧
>
> Make your own smoothies at home! Fill your blender with your favorite frozen fruit. Add juice, milk, or yogurt. Blend and serve!
>
> ✧
>
> Bring leftovers to work for lunch. Nuke them in the microwave, and you have a yummy lunch for free!

will end up in the trash." That is a lot of precious meat that could have been separated into storage bags, stored in the freezer, and used throughout the following months.

Correcting these wasteful ways is a process. It is something we have to learn. I have heard so many people tell me "I don't do leftovers" or "my husband won't eat them." My all-time favorite is, "The kids say no." Well let me give you a bit of advice to shut down this anti-leftover thinking. When it comes to leftovers, you need to get on the bandwagon. I am delivering the memo that leftovers *will* make your life easier and your budget a more realistic thing to follow. You can "do" leftovers, you just need to make the choice to do so.

I know all of this because I used to use these "leftover" excuses. If we didn't finish a meal, then I threw it in the trash. When I cooked, I made a new meal every night. Once I realized all the money I was spoiling by throwing away my extras, I made a change. I realized that leftovers could help me in lowering my grocery budget. If I replaced one meal a week with leftovers, then I could cut quite a bit from my overall grocery budget. Your spouse and kids *will* eat those leftovers.

Although I was ready to become a full-blown leftover supporter, I knew my husband would be a tougher critic. I would have to be creative and trick him. He needed to think he was having a new meal, when in actuality he was eating leftovers.

The first week I decided to use leftovers, I planned out my meal using a lot of things that could cross over into other meals. At the beginning of the week, I cooked a big pork roast with potatoes, carrots, and rolls. After our dinner, I separated the pork roast into three bags full of shredded meat. The next night, we had enchiladas using the shredded pork. The following night, I used it in BBQ sandwiches. I served the meat on the leftover rolls, with the leftover carrots and potatoes as a side dish. The third bag I froze to use the following month. From one pork roast, I was able to get three meals and one freezer meal. Score! I also spent less time preparing my meals each night because a big part of the work was already done. That meant I had more time to spend with my redheads. When I told my hubby how I had tricked him, he was surprised. I had gotten the leader of the anti-leftovers to actually eat and enjoy them. Since then, he has become a staunch leftover supporter.

Make Leftovers Fun

If eating leftovers still seems boring, make it fun. To make leftovers fun, we have family fun leftover nights. I pull all the leftovers out of the fridge. Everyone gets to pick anything they want from the pile of leftovers. My kids love it because they get to choose what they want for dinner. (Those kids love getting any bit of power I give them.) We then all eat in the living room and watch a movie. We made leftovers fun by making it into a family movie night. We save money and spend some precious time together as a family. Get creative. Saving money can be fun!

Crossover Meals

If you can include a crossover meal into your plan, that is an extra bonus! Cooking a whole chicken on Monday in your Crock-Pot gives you a lot to work with throughout the week. You can eat your chicken off the bone the first night, reserving a portion or two for meals later in the week. The second night, you can use that broth—created from cooking your chicken—in a yummy chicken and vegetable soup. The third night, you can use a cup of shredded chicken in a simple rice casserole. The fourth night, you throw it on top of an alfredo pizza. If you still have chicken left, it can be used in quesadillas, chicken casserole, chicken salad, and enchiladas. That one chicken, which you spent about six dollars for, can be stretched into three or four meals. This makes each meal less than two dollars in the meat department. That is an amazing way to make your meat stretch and work for you.

There are many benefits to meal planning. When you meal plan, moments of frustration with cooking will be eliminated, takeout or fast food charges will be avoided, healthier meals will be served to your family, more money will be saved, and mealtime will become a cherished time to converse with family. The stress of the five o'clock blues will be gone. These benefits far outweigh the arguing that can occur as your family decides what fast food place to eat at. No more stress between spouses about escalating credit card bills. I mean really, after reading all that, why would you *not* want to start planning your meals? It brings only positive things into your life.

Dinnertime Is Family Time

This thought came to me one night in bed: I asked myself why everything was so hard. Why did it have to be so hard to get dinner on the table at a responsible hour? Why was it so exhausting being a mom? It was hard because I was making it hard. I am not a perfect mom. I still get frustrated, I still yell a bit too loudly, and I still heave some heavy sighs. Despite all of that, I know that at five o'clock, we will be able to gather around the table and enjoy a meal together. When I look around my kitchen table and see my family enjoying a meal I prepared, my heart is full. There still may be bickering and squabbles, but I did it. I got a healthy dinner into those tummies, and we got to spend a little time together as a family.

Meatless Nights

We all have heard of meatless Mondays, right? It is a huge movement that has been taking place in households across the world. It started in 2003, and since then, celebrities and families alike have been declaring Mondays as their meatless night. Meatless Mondays are a great way for families across the globe to not only save money but also reap some amazing health benefits as well. No matter the day you choose, eating less meat means fewer calories. Those fewer calories mean a reduced intake of saturated fat, lower risk of type 2 diabetes, and a lower risk of heart disease. This easy change can also increase the amount of vitamins, minerals, and fiber you consume.

Going meatless does not mean sacrificing protein. Protein, which is essential to a healthy diet, comes from both animal and plant sources. There are plenty of recipes where you won't miss the meat. Simple dishes like spaghetti and meatballs can be made meat free. Cut out the meatballs and enjoy a meatless meal of homemade spaghetti. Your whole family will love it! Another great way to substitute meat is by adding beans. Beans are inexpensive to buy. I buy mine in twenty-five–pound bags for under eighteen dollars. These last my family a whole year. By substituting beans and legumes for the meat in your favorite dishes, you will save your family money every single month.

One meatless meal each week will make your wallet healthier as well. Meat products are usually the most costly items in your grocery basket. Going meatless just one day per week reduces grocery bills each week.

Meal planning has been a lifesaver to me, and I know it can be for you too. Make dinnertime a bit easier by planning ahead and getting organized.

Frugal Recipes

The recipes on the following pages are some of my family's favorites. They are recipes that I use every day. From our homemade pancake syrup to our homemade bread, your family is sure to love them. From my family to yours, happy cooking!

(These meals serve families of four, with leftovers.)

Maple Syrup

1 cup sugar
1 cup brown sugar
1 cup water
2 Tbsp. butter or margarine
1 tsp. maple flavoring
½ tsp. vanilla

Bring sugars and water to a boil, stirring constantly. Add butter. Cook and stir for 2–3 minutes. Remove from heat and add maple flavoring and vanilla. Stir to combine. I store my leftover syrup in my fridge, in a mason jar. You can serve it cold or reheat it in the microwave for 45 seconds. Warm syrup is just too good!

Buttercream Frosting

⅓ cup butter, softened
¼ cup cream or milk
1 tsp. vanilla
4 cups powdered sugar

Place butter and milk in a mixing bowl. Mix for about 1 minute. Add vanilla and 1 cup powdered sugar. Mix until creamy. Slowly add the remaining powdered sugar, scraping sides of the bowl and mixing as you do. Add additional milk, if needed.

THRIFTY TIPS AND TRICKS

- *This is my go-to icing recipe. It is great on cinnamon rolls, cupcakes, sugar cookies—you name it!*
- *By going homemade, you save money and nix the high fructose corn syrup, which is found in most store-bought kinds.*
- *I like to keep a stock of about six packages of powdered sugar in my freezer to save space and extend the shelf life of the sugar. Just set out on the counter an hour before using it. I do the same thing for my brown sugar.*
- *Keeping a stock of sugars means I am ready to make my family a treat anytime during the month. They are always appreciative.*

Homemade Whipped Cream

1 cup heavy whipping cream
¼ cup sugar

Place both ingredients in the bowl of a stand mixer. Start on low speed. You want to start off slow so you don't get cream splattering out of your bowl. Work up through the speed levels. As your whipped cream thickens, gradually increase the speed of the mixer. Once thick peaks begin to form, your cream is finished. Your whipped cream should be light, fluffy, and oh so delicious!

THRIFTY TIPS AND TRICKS

- *This recipe can be made with a hand mixer too.*
- *Each month, I purchase two half-gallon containers of whipping cream from my local bulk food store. These last us all month. I use them to make whipped cream, caramel sauce, soups, ice cream, and such. Buying my cream in bulk is a huge money saver!*

Caramel Sauce

½ cup butter
2 cups brown sugar
1 cup corn syrup
1 can (14 oz.) sweetened condensed milk
1 tsp. vanilla

Over low heat, melt butter in a saucepan. Next, add your brown sugar and corn syrup. Mix well. Add sweetened condensed milk. Simmer 10–15 minutes, stirring frequently. Continue to stir until sugar is dissolved completely. Remove from heat and add vanilla.

Homemade Vanilla Ice Cream

¾ cup sugar
2 cups heavy whipping cream
1 cup 2-percent milk
1 tsp. vanilla extract

Whisk together all ingredients until combined. Transfer to your ice cream maker. Make according to your manufacturer's directions.

THRIFTY TIPS AND TRICKS

* *Leave your ice cream bowl in the freezer at all times. This allows you to make ice cream whenever the craving strikes. In the summer, we like to celebrate Ice Cream Sundays. This means every Sunday, we make a new kind of homemade ice cream. It is fun for everyone and is a great family activity!*

Foolproof Dark Chocolate Fudge

3 cups semisweet chocolate chips
1 (14-oz.) can sweetened condensed milk
½ cup chopped walnuts
1½ tsp. vanilla extract

Line an 8- or 9-inch square pan with foil. Grease the foil and set aside. In a heavy saucepan, over low heat, melt chocolate chips with sweetened condensed milk. Remove from heat and stir in nuts and vanilla. Spread evenly in prepared pan. Chill 2 hours or until firm. Turn fudge onto a cutting board; peel off foil and cut into squares. Store covered in your fridge.

THRIFTY TIPS AND TRICKS

* *You can do so much with this fudge! Add marshmallows, cherries, or candy pieces for fudge with a flare.*

Apple Pie Brownies

½ cup butter or margarine
1 cup sugar
1 tsp. vanilla
1 egg, beaten

1½ cup flour
½ tsp. baking soda
½ tsp. baking powder
½ tsp. nutmeg
1½ cup apple pie filling
½ cup chopped walnuts

In a large mixing bowl, beat together butter and sugar until fluffy; stir in vanilla and egg. In a small bowl, combine flour, baking soda, baking powder, and nutmeg. Add flour mixture to butter mixture. Mix well. Next, fold in apple pie filling and nuts. Spread batter into a 9×9 baking pan. Bake at 350° for 35–40 minutes. Cool and cut into squares.

THRIFTY TIPS AND TRICKS

- *We love this treat topped with homemade whipped cream and a bit of drizzled caramel sauce. Making both of these homemade is not only a great way to save your family money, but it is healthier too!*
- *Don't have any eggs on hand? No worries! Substitute 1 tablespoon flaxseed and 3 tablespoons water for 1 egg.*

Homestyle Chocolate Chip Cookies

2¼ cups flour
1 tsp. baking soda
1 tsp. salt
1 cup (2 sticks) butter, softened
¾ cup granulated sugar
¾ cup brown sugar
1 tsp. vanilla extract
2 large eggs
2 cups semisweet chocolate chips

Mix the flour, baking soda, and salt together and set aside. Beat butter, sugars, and vanilla in large mixing bowl until creamy. Add eggs. Next, add in flour mixture. Mix well. Stir in chocolate chips. Drop by rounded tablespoons onto baking sheets. Bake 9–11 minutes or until golden brown. Cool on baking sheets for 2 minutes. Remove to wire racks and cool completely.

THRIFTY TIPS AND TRICKS

- *Using a greased tablespoon is a great help for spooning dough onto cookie sheets.*

- *I make these cookies at least once a week. My redheads and hubby gobble these things up. Since I don't buy cookies from the store, I always try to have a filled cookie jar. It makes everyone happy.*
- *Go eggless by substituting your eggs with 2 tablespoons flaxseed and 6 tablespoons water.*

Light and Fluffy Pancakes

1 cup flour
2 Tbsp. sugar
2 tsp. baking powder
½ tsp. salt
1 egg
1 cup milk
2 Tbsp. oil

Place all ingredients in a large mixing bowl. Mix together. Your batter will be slightly lumpy. Pour batter onto a greased hot griddle. I like to use a ¼ measuring cup to make all my pancakes the same size. When the sides of your pancakes get bubbly and the edges are slightly dry, flip to cook other side. Cook on both sides until golden. Serve with homemade maple syrup. Yum!

Basic Dinner Rolls

¾ cup water
2 eggs
3 Tbsp. coconut oil
3 Tbsp. sugar
1 tsp. salt
3½ cups flour
2¼ tsp. yeast

Put all ingredients in your bread machine, according to your manufacturer's directions. Mine go in the order listed above. Select the dough setting. At the end of the program, punch down dough, and let it rest for 5 minutes. Next, pull apart small sections to make balls (make them a little bigger than golf balls). Place them on a greased 9×13 baking dish. You will place rolls 3 across and 12 down to a pan. I put a pad of butter on each roll (apply generously). This butter melts into the roll as it bakes and is absolutely divine! Let rise 15–20 minutes. Bake at 375° 20–25 minutes.

Thrifty Tips and Tricks

- *You can replace the coconut oil in this recipe with butter or vegetable oil. Coconut oil is a pantry staple in my home because it has a great shelf life. It also adds a bit of sweetness to rolls, cookies, and cakes.*
- *I purchase my coconut oil from my local bulk food store. It is under twenty-two dollars and lasts months!*
- *Coconut oil is a multipurpose staple as well! It can be used for skin and hair care too!*
- *You can make these rolls ahead of time and freeze them.*

Eggless Cinnamon Rolls

Why eggless? Well sometimes, at the end of the month, I am running low on supplies and still have a few more days till my next shopping trip. Having a few eggless options (like these cinnamon rolls and my eggless chocolate chip cookies) helps stretch the groceries through the month. I like to make these on Sunday. We then have leftover cinnamon rolls throughout the week for breakfast. This makes getting breakfast on the table a bit easier for me during the week. These would make for a quick breakfast for littles before school. Pair it with some fruit salad, and you're golden!

¾ cup and 6 Tbsp. water
2 Tbsp. flaxseed
3 Tbsp. unsalted butter or margarine
6 Tbsp. sugar
1 tsp. salt
3½ cup flour
2¼ tsp. dry active yeast

Filling

3 Tbsp. butter or margarine, melted
⅓ cup brown sugar
½ Tbsp. cinnamon
raisins (optional)

Put all ingredients into your bread machine, according to your manufacturer's directions. Select manual/dough cycle. At the end of the program, punch down dough and let it rest for 5 minutes.

Roll dough out on a lightly floured surface. Roll out into a rectangle (about 9×10").

Brush rectangle of dough with butter. Next, mix brown sugar and cinnamon in a bowl. Sprinkle onto your dough and rub in. Add a handful of raisins, if desired. Tightly roll your dough into a cylinder. Cut 2-inch pieces and place into a greased 9×13 baking pan, cut side down. Any leftover rolls can go into another greased pan. Recipe makes about 12–14 rolls (depending on how thick you make them). Bake at 350° 20–25 minutes. You want them to be lightly golden brown around the edges. Top with buttercream icing and enjoy!

THRIFTY TIPS AND TRICKS

- *If you don't have flaxseed and want to use eggs, replace the 6 tablespoons of water and 2 tablespoons of flaxseed with 2 eggs in this recipe.*

Pizza Dough

2¼ tsp. yeast
1 tsp. sugar
¾ cup warm water
1¾ cups flour
1 Tbsp. olive oil
½ tsp. salt

Put yeast, sugar, and water in a bowl. Mix until combined. Allow to sit for 5 minutes or until yeast mixture starts to bubble. Add flour, oil, and salt. Mix until a ball of dough forms. Knead for about 5 minutes. Allow it to rest for a few minutes. Next, roll out dough into a circle (size will depend on your pizza pan). Top with your favorite sauce and toppings. Bake 8–10 minutes at 500°.

Homemade Hot Dog and Hamburger Buns

3½ cups warm water
¾ cup oil
¾ cup sugar
6 Tbsp. dry active yeast
1 Tbsp. salt
3 eggs
10–12 cups flour
butter and sesame seeds for topping

Take your first four ingredients and mix in a large mixing bowl or stand mixer bowl. Let sit for 10 minutes. After 10 minutes, your yeast mixture will have doubled in size and will be nice and foamy.

Next, add 1 tablespoon salt, eggs, and 4 cups flour. Mix well. You will start to have a sticky dough. Continue to add 1 cup of flour at a time until the dough pulls away from the side of the bowl. By the eighth or ninth cup of flour, my dough is too big for the bowl, so I flour my counter and begin kneading my dough there. Continue to add flour until your dough is no longer sticky. Your dough should be smooth and elastic. You want to be able to poke it without having the dough stick to your finger. Continue kneading 5–10 minutes.

This recipe requires little rise time, so once your dough is nice and smooth, you can start forming the buns. Pull chunks of dough from your dough bowl. Roll chunks into balls. (You want these to be slightly smaller then the palm of your hand.)

Place your dough balls on greased cookie sheets. Top with melted butter and sesame seeds. Let rise for 10 minutes. Bake at 425° 12–15 minutes. Tops should be golden brown.

This recipe makes 18–20 buns. Once the buns have baked and cooled, you can freeze them in quantities of four. These are great to have throughout the month. Take them out a few hours before dinner, and you will have homemade goodness for your family come dinnertime.

Thrifty Tips and Tricks

- *You don't want your water too cold or too hot. If it is too cold, it will not activate the yeast. If your water is too hot, it could kill the yeast. Using warm water straight from the tap is a perfect option.*
- *Looking for a healthier option? Do a mixture of half white flour and half whole wheat flour.*

Whole Wheat Bread Sticks

2¼ tsp. yeast
1 tsp. sugar
¾ cup warm water
1¾ cups whole wheat flour
½ tsp. salt
2 Tbsp. butter
2 tsp. garlic salt
2 tsp. dried parsley

Combine yeast, sugar, and water in a bowl. Mix until combined. Let the mixture sit for 5 minutes or until the yeast starts to get bubbly. Next, add flour and salt. Mix until a ball of dough forms. Knead for about 5 minutes. Let it rest for a few minutes. Next, roll out dough into an 8×8 rectangle. Take a pizza cutter or knife and cut strips of dough. Place on a greased baking sheet. Melt your butter in a small bowl in the microwave. Brush onto bread sticks. Next, sprinkle top of bread sticks with garlic salt and parsley. Bake 8–10 minutes at 500°.

- *You can use whole wheat flour, white flour, or a combination of both.*
- *These are a great addition to any meal. We especially love these on spaghetti night!*
- *Making homemade breads rather than the store-bought versions is a healthier option for you and your family. You know exactly what is going into your tummies, it tastes delicious, and it costs a heck of a lot less!*

Buttermilk Bread

⅓ cup water
1 cup buttermilk
2 Tbsp. butter or vegetable oil
1½ tsp. salt
4 Tbsp. brown sugar
3 cups flour
2¼ tsp. yeast
4 Tbsp. gluten (optional)

Put all ingredients in your bread machine, according to your manufacturer's settings. Mine go in the order listed above. Select dough setting. Mine takes about 1 hour and 30 minutes. Once your dough cycle is finished, punch down the dough and place it in a greased loaf pan. Put plastic wrap over the top, and wait for it to rise. It should rise above the edges of the pan. Once doubled in size, bake at 350° for 30 minutes or until lightly brown on top. Take out of the oven and immediately rub a cold stick of butter over the top to lightly coat it. Let cool a few minutes and then remove from pan and onto a plate, where it will completely cool. This bread is so yummy when it is served warm with butter and jelly. It is also fantastic for sandwiches!

Thrifty Tips and Tricks

- *Make your own buttermilk by adding 1 tablespoon vinegar or lemon juice to milk. Let it sit for five minutes. The vinegar or lemon juice will cause the milk to turn into buttermilk. Easy peasy!*

Salsa Chicken

3–4 chicken breasts, thawed
1 jar salsa (16 oz.)
1 cup black beans
1 can corn, drained

Place chicken breasts in the bottom of a Crock-Pot. Top with salsa, beans, and corn. Cook on low 5–6 hours. Serve over white rice with a dollop of sour cream.

BBQ Chicken Sandwiches

3–4 chicken breasts, thawed
1 bottle BBQ sauce (18 oz.)

Place chicken in a Crock-Pot. Pour BBQ sauce over chicken. Cook on low 5–6 hours. Shred chicken with a fork. Serve on hamburgers buns.

Slow Cooker Creamy Chicken and Mushrooms

4–6 chicken breasts, thawed
2 (10¾-oz.) cans cream of mushroom soup
½ Tbsp. garlic powder
salt and pepper
1 (4 oz.) can sliced mushrooms
8 oz. cream cheese
½ cup chopped celery

Place chicken in the bottom of a slow cooker. In a small mixing bowl, combine soup, seasonings, mushrooms, softened cream cheese, and celery. Mix well. Pour over chicken. Cook on high 5–6 hours. Serve over rice or pasta.

THRIFTY TIPS AND TRICKS

- *To save yourself time, place frozen chicken breasts in a ziplock bag and then in a sink full of cold water. Change the water every thirty minutes to keep it cold. Go about your morning, and your chicken will be thawed in no time.*
- *When celery is ninety-nine cents per bunch, I like to stock up. Once home, I wash and chop it. Place in a freezer-safe bag or container and freeze. Now you have celery all month long! Throw into casseroles, soups, chicken and turkey salads, or other Crock-Pot dishes. Stocking up and freezing allows you to never run out of celery.*

NOTES

1. Georgina Gustin, "What Leftovers? Many of Us Are Throwing the Feast Away," *St. Louis Post-Dispatch*, November 23, 2012, http://www.stltoday.com/news/local/metro/what-leftovers-many-of-us-are-throwing-the-feast-away/article_ab9f7544-3403-5111-8845-1cd2badb28e9.html.

Chapter 6

Getting Out of Debt and Staying Out

At one time or another, we will all find ourselves paying something off. It could be a smaller debt, like those braces your son needed, or that dentist bill when you had a major cavity. It could also be a major debt like a home, car, or a credit card balance. Most of us will go through this numerous times in our lives. Life is expensive and can have unexpected twists. Don't we all just love those curveballs life sends us? They can be disheartening when we have been struggling to get our finances under control. Those curveballs can make any well-thought-out budget go *kaboosh* in a matter of moments. Having a plan for when debt happens is vital to your frugal journey. Debt can add up quickly. That means we can find ourselves in a whole lot of red before we even blink. Whether you have accumulated a little bit of debt or you are swimming in it, know that you can find a way out of it.

I have learned this firsthand in my own life. There have been times when I felt like my family was drowning in debt. Over time, I have learned the basics for paying down debt. These tips have stuck with me, and I have used them over and over again. No matter the size of your debt, you can follow these simple steps and rid yourself from debt bondage.

Admit That You're in Debt

To start out, as with any addiction recovery program, you need to first admit that you have a problem. I know this may seem like a basic idea, but you'd be surprised how many people I have talked to who swear they are not in debt, but you later find out they are thousands of dollars in the hole because they owe to one credit card company or another. Debt is a big deal. We live in a world that tells us we can have what we want now and pay for it later. More and more people are following this line of thought and end up drowning in their unmanageable debt. We are even told that debt is a necessary evil in our day, but I do not agree. This line of thinking is often used to justify overspending and continuous borrowing. Although we sometimes may need to go into debt to reach a certain goal—like purchasing a modest home, car, or to pay for schooling—it is not a way of life. Using the excuse that everyone is in debt only enables people to dig themselves further into it.

Even if we have accepted that this is a way of life (it doesn't have to be), it is not fun knowing that you owe money to someone. It bogs us down and causes stress to seep into our lives. When I was in debt, I was oblivious to it at first. I had justified my purchases to such a great extent that I truly didn't believe I had a problem. It wasn't until the credit card bills were coming in the mail and I didn't have enough to pay things off that reality hit. I was in debt, and it was no fun. One day, my husband asked me if it made me happy. I thought on this for a while. I loved shopping and being able to score that deal I had been looking for, but I wasn't happy that I was in debt. I realized that, just like any addiction, I was looking for a high. Like any person who has been addicted to gambling, alcohol, or drugs, shopping addicts use that temporary high they get from spending to escape whatever is bothering them. Once I admitted I had a problem, I was able to work toward changing it.

Know Why You Accumulated the Debt

Knowing why you have debt is important so you can change the behavior. If you have debt from frivolous spending, be aware of that so you can prevent it from happening again. Know why you spend the money you do. As I mentioned earlier, my debt started accumulating when my husband was deployed. I was living with family and missing him. As I mentioned, we had many long overseas conversations, but the lightbulb went on for both of us the day he asked me if I was shopping and overspending because I missed him. That tender question made me realize what was really behind my shopping. I'm so grateful that he was patient enough to look for the real problem rather than just being angry with me for the symptom of the problem. I was going through a lot at the time, and shopping became a way to get away from the day-to-day problems I was facing. I can now look back and see what I was doing, but at the time

I was blissfully unaware. He loved me enough to help me figure it out.

Once I came to the realization of why I was overshopping, I knew I had to find another way to bring control into my life. I realized that if I put the same effort I used with shopping into managing my family's finances, I could have that stability and control I so desperately needed. This is what I started focusing on, and amazingly things got better!

Change Your Behavior

When I decided to change the way I was handling stress, I had to go through a sort of detox. Shopping had become my vice. I needed to figure out another way to handle things when life became stressful. This meant, where shopping was concerned, I had to stop cold turkey. There were certain stores I couldn't go to because the temptation to spend was far too great. I admitted that I had limitations and that I only had so much self-control at the time. I took my credit cards out of my wallet so I wouldn't be tempted to use them. To prevent myself from adding further damage to our finances, I locked the credit cards away. Literally. I took them out of my wallet and locked them in a safe. What a freeing thing that was! I no longer had them tempting me to do what I so desperately didn't want to. Just like how an alcoholic wouldn't keep a bottle of liquor in a kitchen cabinet, I couldn't keep the cards in my wallet where I could access them easily. If you know that you have a problem, take the temptation away. Most financial advisors would encourage you to cut up the cards altogether. My baby step was just to put them out of sight, and I felt safer knowing I could turn to them in a true emergency, which helped eliminate the sense of panic I might have felt otherwise.

When I felt stir-crazy at home, I would go for a walk to the park or I would go to the library with the kids. It was a simple change, but it made

Debt Myth: "I have too much debt, so I'll just declare bankruptcy and start over again."

I have talked to many people who find themselves in a lot of debt. These people are usually turning to bankruptcy as a saving grace. Filing bankruptcy will not save you from your problems. Often, people end up in the same financial situation they were in prior to filing bankruptcy because they never dealt with the problems that landed them in debt originally. If you do not change your habits and work on budgeting, then you will soon find yourself back in the same poor financial position.

a huge impact. I wasn't spending money when I was stressed, and I got to spend more quality time with my redheads. It was a better situation all around.

As my behavior changed, something else did too. Because I was spending more time at the library with the kids, I started learning some new skills. I would check out cookbooks, craft books, and historical fiction (my favorite). I hadn't realized how much free time I had when I wasn't always shopping. It was amazing! I started learning how to sew and cook, things that I am now so grateful I was able to learn. I learned how to make bread, and I even created a blog. I had found a love for my old passion of creating. My self-confidence grew. Hubby came home to a new and improved version of me. It was amazing!

It Doesn't Affect Only You

I know most people feel having debt is expected in this day and age, but the simple fact of the matter is that debt is an uncaring master and will follow you every place you go. Placing yourself into debt is willingly putting yourself into financial bondage. The only way to release those chains is by paying it off. Now, I don't mean to sound extreme, but I feel that the more we can understand what debt does to us, the more we will understand why we should want no part of it. Debt doesn't affect just you. It also affects your loved ones. I have seen numerous families greatly burdened by debt. It affects marriages and relationships. It can cause stress and arguments where harmony had existed before. It is often the main downfall of many otherwise healthy marriages.

Attack Your Debt

Once I changed my behavior, I was able to start attacking my debt. I didn't just want to slowly pay off my debt; I wanted to attack it with great ferocity. My phone conversations with Hubby were no longer spent with me making excuses for the things that were going on in my life, but rather

> *Debt Myth:*
> *"It takes forever to pay off debt."*
>
> *I know that many people feel this way when it comes to paying down debts. In fact, I used to think the same thing. When we look at a large amount of debt, it can seem quite impossible to envision ourselves paying it down. It only takes forever if you only pay the minimum on your current debt and continue to accrue new debt. If you are serious though, and attack that debt, then it can be paid down quickly. All it takes is a little discipline and strict budgeting.*

were filled with hopes and dreams. We were able to start planning for a better future because I was no longer spending our savings on frivolous things. We spent many nights talking on the phone about our financial future. We made a plan together so we could battle our debt and come out victorious.

I continued to read *America's Cheapest Family* again and again. Steve and Annette Economides brought light into this dark corner of my life. Through my studying and planning with Hubby, I learned that people are often unsuccessful in attacking their debt and managing their finances because they do not have a rock-solid plan to help them do so. Having a plan, like all things mentioned in this book, is key to ridding yourself of debt, controlling your finances, and living a happier, healthier life. I wanted this for my family.

To pay off our debt, we used the snowball strategy. This enabled us to pay our debts off as quickly as possible. Essentially, the snowball strategy involves making a minimum payment on each of your debt payments *except* the creditor you owe the least to. You attack that debt with all you've got, then work your way up to your larger debts. Starting off small is great because it allows you to build momentum. It also enables you to gain confidence as you pay down your debt. If you were to start with the largest debt first, you may feel defeated before you even begin. Starting off small is a great way to start attacking your debt. To use the snowball strategy, follow a few simple steps:

1. *List your debts.* To attack your debt head-on, you must first know what your debts are. On a sheet of paper or a spreadsheet on your computer, list all of your debts. Start with the smallest balance and work your way up to the largest. Do not worry about the interest rates unless you have two debts with the same payoff balance. When this happens, list the one with the highest interest rate first.

2. *Make minimum payments.* Know what the minimum payment is for all of your debts, and write that down next to your list of debts. Knowing those minimum payments will help you in step 3. Remember that not all debt minimum payments are twenty-five dollars. It depends on the amount of debt on each account. If you don't know, call the financial institution handling your debt and ask.

3. *Attack that debt.* Now that you know what your debt is and what those minimum payments are, you can attack your debt. I am talking *serious*

attacking, people. You want to do it grizzly style. (Hopefully that painted a more accurate picture of what I mean when I say *attack*).

4. *Move on.* Pay the *minimum* payment on all of your debts, except the smallest one. For the sake of illustration, let's say I owe payments to three different credit cards: I owe the first card one hundred dollars, the second two hundred dollars, and the third three hundred dollars. We are going to attack the one hundred-dollar credit card debt first. It represents the first little snowball, and you're going to pinch every penny and pay as much as you feasibly can toward retiring the balance of that debt. Assuming the minimum monthly payment to my one hundred–dollar credit card debt is twenty-five dollars, it's going to take me about four months to completely pay off that card. (Remember, I locked my credit cards in a safe, so I'm not adding to the balance by making new purchases). Each month, for the next four months, I pay just the minimum balance on all three of my credit cards, but after month four, the balance on the first card is paid down to zero, and that debt is gone.

Once that smallest debt is paid, take *all* the money you were paying to that creditor, and add it to the minimum payment owed to the next debt. In this case, assuming my two hundred-dollar credit card debt also has a minimum balance of twenty-five dollars per month, now I can start paying fifty dollars per month to retire that debt until it is all paid off. I'll still be accruing interest, but in four more months, I'll be able to pay off that entire two hundred-dollar balance (plus a little bit of interest that will have accrued) and start adding an extra fifty dollars to the minimum payments I owe on my three hundred–dollar credit card debt.

5. *Keep on.* Keep this up until all debts are paid for. As we pay off debts, I like to keep the total next to the debt in our budgeting spreadsheet. It is really fun to see how each month the car loan goes down or the house loan gets smaller. Celebrate each time it gets under another thousand. Do your own victory dance in the kitchen—you know I do!

Want to know why this system works? It works because it plays to the fact that the majority of people are all about the immediate gratification. We need to know that what we are doing is getting us somewhere. Starting off small and working our way up allows us to celebrate those small victories and see that our hard work is paying off.

While you are paying down your debts, you will want to build a reserve as well. Treat your reserve as another bill you must pay each month. As long as you are consistently adding to it, it will increase and benefit your family. When you set up your budget, decide how much of your extra money you will put toward paying off your debts and how much you will add to your reserve. This will allow you to save a bit while still attacking those debts.

Getting and Staying Out of Debt

Once you have gotten yourself out of debt, it is important not to get yourself right back into it. We should avoid debt at all costs. There is nothing that will cause greater tensions in life than grinding debt. That is why changing our behavior is so important. I have seen many families work hard to get out of debt, only to find themselves back in it a year later. We must change our attitudes and behavior toward money so we can succeed.

Use credit cards only for absolute emergencies once your reserve has been used. Be modest in your spending when you have to use credit. Pay off your debt as quickly as possible. Anytime Hubby and I have accrued some debt, we always go back to the five steps above. The plan makes it manageable to get ourselves out of debt.

Debt Myth:
"A few more charges won't hurt."

Wrong, lovelies! W-R-O-N-G! A few more charges will hurt big time. Adding to your current debt will increase your overall debt payment and will add time to how long it takes for you to pay it all off. Just a few more charges can cost you a lot more than you realize. The sooner you put those credit cards down, the faster you can get yourself out of debt.

Paying off the House

We've all heard the phrase, right? "Bigger is always better." Well, this seems to be an epidemic of thinking that is making its way throughout our nation. So many people want more and more. In the past forty years, house sizes have skyrocketed. What once was considered a modest home in the 1970s is now considered minuscule in today's society. What once was perfectly fine for past generations is no longer acceptable to us. The standard home size in 1970 was 1,600 square feet. Over the years, that number has gradually increased as the American dream has grown. The standard house size is now well over 2,600 square feet.[1] In just fifty years, houses have grown to astounding sizes. It seems that as the next generation grows into adulthood, we are left with people who want exactly what their parents worked years and years to obtain. We are living in an entitled generation.

People feel that they are entitled to a big house, a great car, a great job, and so on. So many people want much more than they have. We thrive on instant gratification. We do not want to wait for what we want now. We must be careful in this false thinking. Having bigger and better does not always mean it is "bigger and better." Confused? Let me explain.

You can want that great big house. You know, the two-story house on the corner with the wraparound porch? The house with the great yard and four bedrooms? That house is misleading though. In fact, it is very misleading. Sure, it looks like it is fresh out of a magazine, especially once you add a little flower garden in the front, but what that "bigger and better" house isn't telling you is the trouble it will cause you. You see, that house is a bit out of your price range. It would be quite a stretch to swing it, even though it sure does look good with the white trim and shutters. The house also doesn't tell you how, because it is "bigger and better," it will cost more to keep cool in the summer and warm in the winter. Many people fall into this "bigger is better" thinking and have paid the price over the years.

In early 2006, when the housing market was at an all-time high, many people were buying houses, and they were buying big! People got into loans with high interest rates just so they could score that American dream of a three-bedroom, two-bath home. The only kicker was later that year, housing rates began to decline and continued falling until 2008, when they hit a record low. Many people who had chosen to live beyond their means were hurting financially. The year 2008 brought a recession—a time in American history where people were hurting for jobs. Unemployment was at an all-time high and foreclosures were common. So many people had overstretched their finances, and there was nowhere to go but down.

This was a hard time. I saw good people lose their homes because of poor financial decisions. These people had gotten stuck in the "bigger is better" mind-set, and it had come back to bite them. It is not better if you cannot afford it. This is something to always remember. The "bigger is better" thought process is ingrained in us. We must change our mind-set to break the cycle. We do not need bigger things to live a happy, fulfilled life. It is not better if we are so stretched financially that we would hit rock bottom if we missed a paycheck. Stretching yourself that thin can be quite burdensome and not smart.

L. Tom Perry said, "We think we need a larger home, with a three-car garage, [and] a recreational vehicle parked next to it. . . . We long for designer clothes, extra TV sets, . . . the latest model computers, and the newest car. Often these items are purchased with borrowed money, without giving any thought to providing for our future needs. The result of all this instant gratification is overloaded bankruptcy courts and families that are far too preoccupied with their financial burdens."[2] Elder Perry knew what he was talking about. It is important that we be modest in our choosing of a home so that we are able to live within our means. Choosing to not overstretch ourselves will allow us to gain more freedom financially and pay off that house quicker.

I have compiled a few tips to help you pay off your home. A home loan is one of the biggest loans people take out. Although home debts are large, it is still possible to pay them off. By following a few simple steps, you can pay that home loan off quicker and free up a lot of money for your family to enjoy.

Tips for Paying off Your Mortgage Quicker

1. When you budget for your mortgage, plan to pay half the usual amount every two weeks, instead of the full payment every month. This will result in lower interest charges and an extra mortgage payment at the end of the year. Check with your mortgage lender so you can set up these types of payments.

2. Make one extra mortgage payment a year. It is a simple thing that will make a huge difference. This becomes quite doable when you think of that nice tax return you get each year. Taking a portion of that tax return and putting it toward paying down your home will be money well spent. No one wants to be paying off their house when they are ninety.

3. Add extra money to the principal on every mortgage payment. Adding just twenty or fifty dollars each month toward the principal will make a huge difference!

4. Be wary of refinancing. If you are doing it to get a lower monthly rate so you can put money toward the principal, that may be wise, but remember that every time you refinance, you are extending out that loan end date. Ask yourself if you want to still be paying off a home loan when you're ready to retire. Always weigh the pros and cons.

Keeping up with the Joneses

I couldn't end this chapter without talking about the Joneses. We all love the Joneses, right? Well maybe *love* is a strong word. A lot of times, we just try to keep up with them. On my blog, I often get asked how I don't give in to the "keeping up the Joneses" mentality that seems to be running rampant in our society. I am here today to answer this age-old question. I don't worry about keeping up with the Joneses because they're broke. Seriously! From the outside they look polished and all put together, but for the most part they are struggling financially. They are having trouble keeping themselves together. Many people driving around the suburbs in their giant SUVs and talking on their new cell phones are deeply in debt. If you were to ask them how they are doing, they would tell you that they are just barely getting by. Many have overextended themselves to purchase items on credit because of the need for instant gratification. They may require two incomes to stay afloat and are headed for disaster if one wage earner is ever out of work for an extended period of time. We live in a society that wants everything new and wants it now.

I have worked with many people who have fallen into this "keeping up with the Joneses" mentality, only to regret it later down the road. They find themselves in a great amount of debt, living paycheck to paycheck, wondering where they went wrong. Well, the Joneses went wrong! You need to change your mind-set. It is kind of like rewiring your brain. If you have grown accustomed to living a certain way, whether you could afford it or not, you have made a habit out of it. You need to break that bad habit and change your way of thinking.

Having a "Joneses'" moment is something we all face every now and then. Even a saving diva like me has times when I want to keep up with those Joneses. Sometimes it hits me when I visit a friend's house and see cute wall decor or when I am out shopping. It is easy to get down and feel like all your hard work is not helping because you can't buy those things you so desperately want. It is in these moments that I remind myself that those things I think I need to be happy and enjoy life are just that— *things*. They are objects with price tags that I don't have the budget for. They are not important in my overall life mission. I remind myself of the things I do have. I basically have a "count your many blessings" pep talk with myself. This usually pulls me right out of my Joneses funk.

Now, before anyone gets the wrong idea here, I am not saying having things is bad. I like things just like any other person, but going into debt for those things is not okay. It actually hurts you in the long run, and that feeling of happiness you had when you bought that thing is temporary. Trust this recovering shopaholic. It usually fades by the time you get the bill in the mail and realize how everything you thought you needed added up and has now become a burden. So *things* are not bad, but buying things you do not have the money for is not smart.

Choose to spend more time with your loved ones and less money on them. Remember that it is not the amount of money we spend on the people we love, but rather the time spent that counts. Do not let money matter more than other things in life. We cannot compare ourselves to others, although it is something we often do (especially us ladies). Remember how I talked about that Supermom we create in our heads? We tend to do it with other things too. We see Nancy who has all the cute knickknacks in her house, and we want to have those things too. We see Bill down the street who just bought a new car, and we want one too. We have to stop putting all this financial pressure on ourselves. All those things are just things. They do not hug us when we are sad. They do not make us laugh. We have to make sure that we do not get into the dreaded predicament of keeping up the Joneses. Be happy where you are and relish it. Find contentment in your day-to-day life.

In the grand scheme of things, you will not look back on your life and wish you had spent more money. You will, however, look back and wish you had spent more time with those who mattered most. You will never regret the time enjoyed with your children, parents, friends, and spouses. You will look back on those moments with huge smiles at the joy that was brought into your life because of those precious moments and memories you shared together. Commit to your relationships. They will bring you the greatest satisfaction.

NOTES

1. Mark J. Perry, "Today's new homes are 1,000 square feet larger than in 1973, and the living space per person has doubled over last 40 years," February 26, 2014, http://www.aei.org/publication/todays-new-homes-are-1000-square-feet-larger-than-in-1973-and-the-living-space-per-person-has-doubled-over-last-40-years/.

2. L. Tom Perry, "If Ye Are Prepared Ye Shall Not Fear," October 1995, https://www.lds.org/general-conference/1995/10/if-ye-are-prepared-ye-shall-not-fear?lang=eng.

Chapter 7

A Great Wardrobe on a Budget

I grew up never knowing a thrift store. Thrift stores were only where (*say in a whisper*) poor people went (*gasp*). I had absolutely no clue. I had created this stigma around thrift stores. I thought them to be dirty, unorganized, and full of broken junk no one wanted. In my naive, young mind, I couldn't believe that people actually shopped at thrift stores, let alone found treasures! You donated to them, but you never shopped at them, or at least that is what I thought. If I could go back, I would give my younger self a good talking to. Sometimes I think we have to look back and see our shortcomings. By doing this, we can see what things we would like to change within ourselves. I looked down my nose at all of that thrifting mumbo jumbo because I couldn't see the possibilities. All I saw was junk that people didn't want anymore. The whole "buy used and save the difference" concept was foreign to me. If only my sixteen-year-old self could see me now. She'd be staring, her mouth open in astonishment. I've definitely turned around since my younger years.

About eight years ago, I entered my first thrift store. We were living in Washington, and my mother-in-law had come for a visit. She is an avid thrift store shopper and convinced me to check out a store just down the street from my apartment. She felt it was destiny we venture out and try it on for size. I was hesitant. Okay, I was *really* hesitant. I still had that dirty thrift store picture painted in my head. I just didn't think thrift stores and I would get along, but that sweet mother-in-law of mine thought otherwise, so I brought along some hand sanitizer, and we set off.

I honestly thought I would hate it, but I was pleasantly surprised. I saw row after row of clothes with so much promise. For the first time in my life, I saw potential in a secondhand item. My eyes were beginning to open to the world of thrifting. To say my mother-in-law was pleased was an understatement. She's a thrifter from way back, so the more people she can convert to thrifting, the better. Throughout the years, she has helped encourage my love for frugality.

While in that initial thrift store, I saw toys that had once been loved but now waited for new little owners. I fell in love. I couldn't believe what my sixteen-year-old self had been missing out on. Thrift stores were pretty darn awesome! The colors in my thrift store painting began to change. I no longer saw drab grays and blacks. I saw colors of vibrant hues. I purchased a few "new to us" toys and clothes for my family that day. I spent a few dollars on a gently used Barbie Jeep for my daughter and a bag of cars for my boy. I was able to purchase things for my family for a fraction of the "new in store" price. I was astounded.

Now fast-forward a few years. I was back in Nevada and living with my mother-in-law. Hubby was in that desert in Iraq, and I was out of control. Forgetting the brief love affair I had established with thrift stores, I had convinced myself that if I bought it on clearance, I was saving our family money. I forgot that I wasn't saving us money if I bought something we didn't need. It was at this time that I had the rock-bottom moment we've already talked about and realized I needed to change the way I was living. Slowly, our family mantra became "buy used and save the difference." We now try to follow it in everything we do.

Starting Out

I have mentioned that when I decided to stop shopping, I had to do it cold turkey. I got up one morning and said, "Danielle, you will not buy anything new. You will only buy what you *need,* and you will be conscious of everything you bring home." I had to remind myself of this daily. If the shopping monster wanted to come out, I would repeat those words in my head. I had to be the change I wanted to see within my own little world. I had control over the way I was living. I could no longer hide behind my justifications.

Since I was going to commit to buying things secondhand, I knew I would need to learn a few domestic skills. I asked my mother-in-law to teach me how to sew. I had a sewing machine but had no clue how to use it. That sweet lady taught me the ins and outs of it. I still remember the first thing I sewed. It was a dress for my daughter. I made it out of a pillowcase I found at a thrift store for one dollar. After that dress, I was hooked. I had always been a crafty person, but somewhere along the way, I had lost that spark. As I started creating things again, using only my ingenuity and a few thrift store supplies, I finally felt like I had it back. Choosing to live on a budget and changing the way I shopped forced me to think outside the box. It pushed me to be more creative. I am thankful for that. I learned that there is joy and happiness in being able to create something out of basically nothing.

Set a Budget

I know, I know! It's the *b* word again. How many times can I tell you to set a budget in this book? More times than I can count! It truly is the foundation of any well-thought-out plan. No matter your income, you should decide how much you'll spend on clothing each month. This will become a category in your budget. Putting aside money each month for clothing allows you to have the money always ready when clothing needs arise. Decide as a family what you can realistically set aside for clothing. You may not use it every month. Some months you may save fifty dollars and other months only ten dollars. As long as you are consistently putting a little aside each month, you will be able to have the funds needed when a child grows out of his or her shoes and the purchase becomes a *need* instead of a want.

Setting aside money every month does not mean you have to spend it. It means you are thinking ahead and saving for the day when you will need it. There are many months when I do not buy any clothes at all. During those months, the money set aside is saved. This allows me to take advantage of sales when they happen, because I know the money has already been allocated and is accumulating. Every year, I look forward to two big clothing trips—one in March and one in September. During these two months, a local thrift store has a half-off sale on all clothing. I am usually able to get clothes for our family for under $150. With pants and shirts under $2, clothing my family for less than $150 is quite doable. With some smart planning and shopping, I am able to spend less on the clothing my family uses every day.

Take Inventory

I think it is important to take inventory of what you already have in your closet. This is a good thing to do before you go clothing shopping.

Just like we take stock of our pantry before we grocery shop, we should do the same with our closet. There is no need to get a new pair of jeans just because they are on sale when you already have five pairs at home. While you are taking inventory, it is a good idea to pull things out that you haven't worn in a while. If you are not sure, you can place all clothes with hangers facing the wrong way at the beginning of a season. If at the end of the season you have hangers that haven't been changed, you know you didn't wear that item. Get rid of it.

When we take inventory, is important to be honest with ourselves. Are we holding onto pants because we hope someday we will be able to fit into them? Are we hanging onto a shirt that is too large, because at one point we dropped a pretty penny on it? I was guilty of both of these mistakes. Over time, I learned that having these things in my closet was only taking up space. I want all the items in my closet to be things I love and use often.

Enjoy where you are right now. If you want to lose a few pounds, I support you, but don't let those too-small jeans hanging there make you feel like a failure. Pack them away or give them away to someone else who can use them. If you end up losing the weight, you'll know exactly how to reward yourself on your next shopping trip at the thrift store!

Stay Organized

When Hubby and I got married, we had to combine two different organization styles. Hubby grew up differently than I did. I grew up with a maid, and everything had its place. The bed was made every day, you put your laundry away, and rooms were cleaned before you went to bed. This was a must in my home growing up. Hubby lived in a more relaxed home. My mother-in-law had six kids to chase after, so out of necessity, cleaning and organization were

"Learn to sew! I always alter my kiddos' clothes. I hem pants to shorts or capris and long-sleeved tops and dresses into short-sleeved. By the time winter rolls around, they will have outgrown them. This way they can wear them through the spring and into summer. I also do hand-me-downs. I have some clothes that have lasted me through all four of my girls. I like to get my money's worth."

—Amy M.
(Las Vegas, NV)

"Barter when you can. No one spends money, and everyone wins! Use what you are good at to help someone else: babysitting, photography, minor car repairs, [and so on]."

—Katy D.

sometimes left on the back burner. Because of that, Hubby grew up with his own system for keeping his room tidy. Dirty clothes went into one basket and clean ones in another. When I asked him how he could tell the baskets apart, he sweetly replied, "I smell it." When we got married, we had to find a way to somehow mesh our two styles.

The first thing we did was color-coordinate each side of closet. I know it sounds extreme, but hear me out. There is a method to my madness, which Hubby has now come to appreciate. Color-coding your closet actually makes things work more efficiently. When you get up in the morning and want to quickly pull an outfit together, having things divided by color makes it easy to find what you're looking for. The shelves in our closets are used for holding folded pants and sweaters as well. Taking advantage of all the space and keeping things tidy makes it easier on everyone.

Shop the Sales

You didn't know thrift stores have sales? They do! Check out where your local thrift stores are. Some of the more popular ones are Deseret Industries, Salvation Army, Goodwill Industry International, and Savers. There are loads of local thrift stores too! Check the yellow pages or Google it. You never know what little gems will be located near you. A local thrift store that I love sends me weekly emails. They let me know what their tag sales are that week. This particular store has different colored tags, which go on sale each week. Sometimes they are half off or only one dollar. Taking advantage of thrift-store sales means you get to stretch your money even further! Recently, one of my favorite thrift stores had a purple-tag sale. All clothes with purple tags cost only fifty cents. I was able to score a cute black pencil skirt for under one dollar. I was ecstatic!

Some thrift stores also have military appreciation days, senior discount days, and teacher appreciation days. Ask around to see what deals and sales your local thrift stores have going on. Why not save when you can?

Refashion

The old idiom "Don't judge a book by its cover" applies to clothes as well! Don't take clothing items at face value. Remember, one man's trash is another's treasure. At first you may see an old, frumpy denim jumper, but with a little bit of tweaking, you can create a fun new piece to add to your wardrobe. Think outside the box. I know for some this is more diffi-cult. It is literally rewiring your brain. When I look at clothes, I ask myself a few questions. First, can I wear it as is? Second, do I have something in my closet right now that will work with it? There is no use buying an item you cannot wear right now. Purchasing an item only to have pur-chase three other items to make it an outfit is not saving money. It causes you to spend more. Third, if it is not okay as is, what can I make it into? Too-short dresses can become shirts, sweaters can become cardigans, and pants can become shorts. The options are endless.

I also find fabric and sheets at thrift stores. I use both to create clothes for my daughter and me. A sheet can become a maxi skirt real quick. I also love to look for inspiration via the web, so when I am at a thrift store I can remember projects I have seen on Pinterest. When you have a few refashion ideas in your back pocket, it is much easier to think outside of that dreadful fashion box we put ourselves in. Be creative and one of a kind!

Have a Wish List

Just like when you were little and you circled the toys in the Christ-mas catalog, have a list of things you are looking to incorporate into your wardrobe. Whether it is a mental list or a paper-and-pen list, keep one. I learned this technique a few years ago on a fashion blog. I thought it was absolutely brilliant and decided to start applying it right away. It gave my thrifting more purpose. Now I keep an eye out for those items on my wish list. I know some of you right now are wondering, "Well, isn't it just easier to run to Target and get that item right then?" Sure, it would be easier, but do we always have to have immediate gratification? I had a simple button-down white shirt on my wish list for a long time. When I finally found one, I was so excited! I felt like I had snagged that purple elephant I talked about earlier. Instead of paying close to $20 for a shirt, I was patient and found one for 50 cents. I saved $19.50 by waiting. You can't buy that feel-ing when you finally snag an item you've been searching for. Sometimes the best things take a bit of time, but they are so worth it.

Make Thrifting a Hobby

I know all of you ladies out there are busy. Whether you are a busy mom, wife, worker, or anything else, you deserve a little "me time." Use thrifting to fill that need. When I go to a thrift store by myself, it is like going to Disneyland. I get a little bit of time with me, myself, and I. Thrifting is a passion of mine. I love the feeling of entering a thrift store and scoring the best deal possible. Yes, it takes a bit of time to scour the racks, but it is a time I have come to enjoy. As your kids get older, you can bring them along and make it a hobby for them as well. My little Miss loves to thrift with me. That girl is only seven, but she already has a flare for the frugal. She is super creative and will pull clothes off the rack and let me know what we can make from them. I love that this little hobby of mine is now becoming one for her as well.

Invest in the Basics

When we are building a wardrobe, we want to make sure that we are filling it with things that we not only love but will also stand up to various fads. I always encourage people to "think classic." Classic styles never fade or go out of season.

Also, be aware not to get pulled in by a frugal price tag. Buying a bunch of cheap clothes only to have to replace them each year is not saving you money. Look for quality pieces when you are shopping—pieces that can really contribute to the overall depth of your wardrobe.

I always encourage people to invest in the basics first. I've included a basic wardrobe list for adults and children. Just like with food, if we keep our basics stocked, then we will save ourselves money in the long run because we can do so much more with the basics. When our wardrobe is made up of a lot of eccentric pieces, it becomes harder to make outfits out of them. So start with the basics and work your way up from there.

Wardrobe Basics for Women

1 pair of athletic shoes
1 pair of basic black heels or flats

1 pair of heels or flats in a fun color or pattern
1 pair of sandals in a basic color (I prefer black)
1 basic button-down shirt
7–8 shirts
2–3 cardigans
2–3 skirts
5–6 pairs of pants
2–3 statement necklaces and earrings
seasonal clothes (jacket, hat, gloves, swimsuit)

Wardrobe Basics for Men

1 pair of dress shoes
1 pair of work boots
1 pair of athletic shoes
1 pair of sandals
7–8 shirts
5–6 pairs of pants
2 button-down shirts
1 suit jacket
2 ties (for church or work)
seasonal clothes (jacket, hat, gloves, swimsuit)

When we break it down this way, it makes things a bit simpler. We live in a time of excess. For a lot of us, it starts in our closets. Have you ever looked at the new homes they are building in this country? One of the things that people look at, besides bathrooms and kitchens, are closets. We all want a huge, spacious walk-in closet. I am guilty of this myself. I dream of having a closet I could dance in. The only problem is that as closets get bigger, we tend to think we need to fill them, leaving us with tons of clothes we don't wear. Knowing what the basics are for a wardrobe will help us in know where we are on the clothing front. If we invest first in the basics and go from there, our wardrobe will be the better for it. You want to have quality pieces that can mix and match with one another.

This also gives us a starting point. If we know we already have these items in our closets, then we will be reminded not to overbuy. You can only have so many pairs of jeans and so many button-down shirts. Keeping to the basics in your closet will prevent you from overindulging yourself in whatever store you are shopping at.

When you are shopping for clothes, do it wisely. Look for the sales, and buy only what you need. Just like with food, it is not benefiting you if you buy a bunch of stuff only to have it sit in your closet not being used. When you receive gift cards for holidays or birthdays, use them wisely. Invest in some statement pieces that will complement your current wardrobe, and buy things on sale so you can stretch your money as much as possible. I buy packages of underwear and socks new. Everything else is an opportunity to be wise and make a good investment while paying less for it.

Shop for Charity

I don't have a lot of money. I can't donate as much as I would like to the charities I believe in, but I can use what spending power I have to support a good cause, be green, and look fabulous all at the same time. I can do this all by shopping at charity shops! This idea can completely change the way we consume, and why we consume.

We rarely buy new household items. We'll shop in thrift stores, pawnshops, furniture auctions, and yard sales. We try to get bargains on everything we can. We even buy our cars used because there is such a high depreciation on them. The same goes with furniture. You can get really nice things that are like new because somebody's moving away or doesn't need them anymore. There have been numerous times I have gone into a thrift store and have seen clothes with the tags still on. You've got be willing to wait to get what you are looking for at just the right price.

No matter how you do it, you can look your best on a budget. By shopping smart and thinking ahead, you can clothe your family for only a fraction of what the new in-store cost would be. Think outside the box and get creative!

Ten Money-Saving Tips for Raising Kids

I am always asked how Hubby and I save with our little ones. These money-saving strategies will help you save no matter how large or small your brood is. Having children does not have to send you in a downward spiral of debt. By choosing to do simple, everyday things, you can save money and still have that family you have always wanted.

1. *Buy used and save the difference.* Why pay more if you don't have to? Thrift stores, outlet stores, yard sales, and consignment stores all offer

great prices on used children's clothes and goodies. Buying used will help you plan for baby, without breaking the bank. Accepting hand-me-downs is a great way to save as well. My son lived in hand-me-downs for the first few years of his life. A sweet neighbor had a son who was two years older than our Keagan. She would box up all of her son's outgrown clothes and give them to us. We saved so much by accepting hand-me-downs. When Miss Priss came around, we did the same thing. We now know that with whatever little ones God blesses us with, we do not have to spend a fortune to prepare for their sweet arrival.

2. *If possible, try to nurse.* When you have little ones, try to nurse them as long as possible (twelve to twenty-four months). This will help your family cut down on formula costs. I nursed both of my babies for almost a year. The longer you are able to nurse, the healthier both your wallet and your little one will be.

3. *Go homemade.* When it comes to food for the little ones, the more you can go homemade the better. You can make baby food at home by cooking and pureeing fresh fruits and veggies. I did this before I even decided that living a thrifty lifestyle was cool. You can also make your own rice cereal at home. You only need a half cup of brown rice, four cups of water, and some type of food processor (Baby Bullet, NutriBullet, blender, and so on). Add the uncooked brown rice to the food processor and mill to a fine powder. Add the milled brown rice and four cups of water to a pot and cover until it boils. Then turn the heat to low and cook with the cover for twenty minutes. Check the consistency of the brown rice cereal and add water if you want it to be thinner. Once the cereal is the consistency most suitable for your little one's age, serve immediately or pour it into storage cups and freeze or refrigerate. You can refrigerate for up to three days or freeze for thirty days. This is so much cheaper than store-bought baby food and healthier too! A quarter cup of uncooked rice will yield sixteen ounces of baby food.

4. *Consign or sell clothes and household items you no longer need.* There are so many ways to sell your used items. Consignment stores are a great way to make money on your children's outgrown clothes. A consignment store is a store that sells secondhand items (typically clothing and accessories) on behalf of you, the original owner. The store receives a percentage of the selling price as well. Some consignment stores give you your percentage in

cash, or you can use it to buy more clothes for your little ones. Yard sales are also another great way to sell old clothes and kid items. It's an easy way to sell unused items to neighbors, friends, and yard sale fanatics. There are also a few Facebook pages dedicated to selling and purchasing (just like a yard sale). I live in an area where two Facebook pages are available for me to shop and sell on. This is a great way to buy things at a fraction of the store price. It is also great at Christmastime when you're looking for toys. Check your local area and see what pages are available to you where you can take advantage of selling your unwanted items. Your trash will be someone else's treasure. You can also use Ebay and Craigslist as well.

5. *Shop their closets first.* Every season, my little ones and I spend an afternoon going through their clothes. We usually do this when the seasons are starting to change. I have my children try all their clothes on to see if they still fit. It is amazing the things that they think still fit and try on actually won't. By having my kids try things on, I am able to take stock of what they already have in their drawers and what they have outgrown. In the winter, I check to make sure they have five to six pairs of pants, seven to eight long-sleeve shirts, two hoodies, a winter jacket, plenty of socks and underwear, one or two church outfits, and winter pajamas. Taking stock before I go shopping for a new season saves me tons. Some items may still fit them from the previous winter. This allows me to not over-buy and overspend. Recently, we went through my son's clothes. Before taking inventory of his clothes, I was convinced he would need a whole new winter wardrobe. Once we went through and I wrote down what he had, I realized he already had half the things he needed for the upcoming winter season. I do the same thing in the summer. Any jeans that will not fit them the following winter get turned into shorts. I simply cut them at the desired length and hem the bottoms. This is a great way to stretch their clothing further and not have to buy a brand new wardrobe come summertime. For the summer, I like them to have five to six pairs of shorts, seven to eight short-sleeve shirts, one swimsuit, plenty of socks and underwear, one or two church outfits, and summer pajamas. Once I have taken stock of what they currently have, I wait for the sales. When the seasons change, thrift stores always have great sales to change inventory. Last April, I was able to take advantage of a children's sale my local thrift store was having. I was able to snag five pairs of shorts for my daughter for only fifty cents a pair. I was also able to find some character shirts my daughter I had been looking for, a pair of DC shoes for my boy, and some

fun summer pajamas as well. Taking stock saves my family money every single year!

6. *Teach them needs versus wants.* Teaching our children this crucial lesson is something that will stay with them for years to come. In our family, we want to make sure our children know that we have to work hard to earn a living. We have to put forth the effort to be able to have those things we need to live. Having a safe home, food to eat, and clothes to wear are all necessities of life. Having a huge home, extravagant food, and name-brand clothes are not a need but a want. The more that we can teach our children this, the better off they'll be.

7. *Teach them the importance of saving.* Children in a nutshell are pretty similar to adults when it comes to spending and saving. They all see something and automatically think they need it or want it. Those desires are normal for children and adults alike. It is not a bad thing to want something. When our children come to us telling us they want something, this is a time to teach them about saving up for the things that they want. If it is not their birthday or Christmas, encouraging them to save up for those "fun" things they've seen at the store is a great way to teach them responsibility. It also lets you know if they really want that particular item or not.

A few years ago, our son wanted a new video game. He had played it at a cousin's house and felt that he too must have it. There was only one problem: the game cost fifty dollars. Definitely not in my budget or his. His birthday had just passed, along with Christmas. He had a decision to make. He could wait until next year when Christmas and his birthday rolled around, or he could start saving. He decided on the latter. He pulled weeds for his Nana and Papa and counted all the money he had saved from his birthday. He almost had enough. He was just a few dollars short. Then he had an idea: what if he included his sister in on the fun? She also loved the video game he was saving up for. They decided that they would put their money together to buy the video game. It was such a neat experience to see them work hard for something they wanted. They worked as a team and have had a blast playing that game together. When our children do decide to save up for something, we encourage them to also try to find it at thrift stores and such before buying it new. With some electronics, this can be a bit hard, but by shopping used or taking advantage of a sale, they have learned how they can save their money and still get what they want.

8. *Teach your children contentment.* We try to teach our children to be content with what they been blessed with. We try to drive home the fact that the things that they have are truly blessings from God. There are many children throughout the world who are more worried about where their next meal will come from or whether they will be safe when they sleep at night. As my husband traveled with the military, this was one important lesson he learned. The things that we tend to fret about here are not even on the worry list of people in other countries. We can teach our children to be content with the food and clothing they have and encourage them to use the excess to bless the lives of others and serve God.

9. *Teach them to work.* We don't have to clean our house; we get to clean our house. See how I changed *have* to *get*? I do this often when talking to my children. I want them to know that the things that we do in life are a privilege. Getting to play video games or watching television is not things we *have* to do; they are things we *get* to do. Doing chores, learning in school, and serving others are not things we *have* to do, but rather are blessings we *get* to be part of. The more we teach our children that being able to work and help others is a blessing, the more independent and resourceful we will help them become.

10. *Make it special.* Our children know that Christmas and birthdays are when Mom and Dad buy new things. We think every kid should get something nice for the holidays. We set our budget and shop their wish list. This means that they really think about what they ask for from us. Sometimes they will tell us they want something after seeing a commercial. When that happens, we try to encourage them to think about how they will use that toy or item and if they will really enjoy it. Many times, once they give it more thought, they realize they don't want it as much as they thought they did. This becomes another opportunity to teach our kids to be conscious of what they are asking for and how it will ultimately benefit them. This is a crucial thing to teach them and will benefit them as they get older.

Chapter 8

Family Night

If your family is anything like mine, you feel pulled in many directions. There are jobs to attend to, extracurricular activities to go to, and everything else in between. Life is busy, and some days it can feel downright impossible to find a time when the whole family can sit down and be together. Because life can be so busy, it is important to take time each week to be together as a family. We need to continually strengthen and nurture our family relationships. We want time together where no one is glued to an electronic device or off doing their own thing. We do this by having time where we laugh, talk, and enjoy one another's company. That is what family night is all about. It is about making your family a priority, taking time out of each week to be together, and enjoying those little ones whom we get to love. No matter how busy life may seem, there is always time for family. By prioritizing, getting creative, and having fun, you can enjoy time together.

Why Family Night Is Important

We all come from different family backgrounds. Maybe you were raised in a happy, secure family with loving parents. Maybe you weren't. Maybe growing up for you was tough and left you longing for love and support. No matter what your family upbringing was, know that you have control over what happens in your own family today. No matter where you come from, you can choose to change or enhance the way you were raised. My family had family nights often. Whether we were at the park playing, heading to the lake to swim, or staying up late to watch a movie, it was important that we had time together as a family. Both of my parents worked, so when they had time off, they wanted to make sure they spent it with their children. I am so thankful they did that. By doing that, they were an example to me and let me know how important my brother and I were to them. This has always been something I wanted to do in my own family.

When Hubby and I got married, we found out we were expecting a baby only two months later. We were thrown into that role of parenthood early in our marriage. When I knew a little bean was going to be joining us, I wanted to make sure he knew how important he was to our family, just like my own mother and father had done for me. Schedules can fill up faster than you think, so it is important to plan for time together. Just like those dentist appointments and Church meetings I log into my day planner, I block out time each week for a family night. I do this so that no matter how busy our week may get, we know that Monday night is our night to be together without distractions from work, Church, or those pesky rectangular devices we can't seem to put down. There are so many distractions in this world. Having a night off from those distractions is really a wonderful thing. I love my phone like any other mama out there. I spend a lot of time on social media promoting posts, sharing with readers, and uploading videos onto YouTube. Although I spend a lot of time behind a laptop or my phone, it is a nice reprieve to put it down and forget about whatever update I want to post on Facebook or deadline I need to meet. Instead, I can just hang out with those awesome people I call my family.

It's All about Priorities

When our children are babies, it can seem rather simple to plan fun activities with them. There are not as many errands to run. It is when those munchkins get older and start having activities to be rushed to and school to be picked up from that life gets more interesting.

When our son was eight, we signed him up for wrestling. He was taking mixed martial arts lessons at a local gym and was loving it. He went five days a week, and we had our daughter involved in a ballet and tap class. To say we were busy was an understatement. I felt like a personal chauffeur. Most of my time was spent carting kids from here to there. We would get home late to eat a quick dinner and head off to bed. I felt like we had little time to be together as a family. After a year of this hectic schedule, I realized that I wasn't happy anymore. I missed those cozy evenings at home when we would pull out a board game or we would bake cookies together and talk. I missed my family. I called a family meeting and expressed my concerns with my husband and children. They also agreed. We all missed that time together. We love each other and love spending as much time together as we can. Once we realized we needed to cut back on all of our commitments and make more time for our family, something happened. There were fewer fights, and there was a greater peace in my home. We had been stretching ourselves so thin that we had become a family with a bad case of the grumpies. Once we made sure our family was a priority, things got better.

Learn to say no when you are stretched too thin. Learn to say yes to those littles. Say yes to going to the park, say yes to snuggles on the couch, say yes to long car rides and late-night chats. Make the things that you value most the things you put the most time into.

Using Family Night to Bring You Closer

In our home, we like to use family night as a time to study and strengthen our love for the scriptures and our Father in Heaven. On Monday nights, we always get together at six o'clock for a scripture lesson. It only takes about fifteen minutes. Someone shares a gospel message or teaches a quick lesson on something from the scriptures. We like to keep it short and sweet because we know kids have pretty short attention spans. The main goal is to share our religious beliefs and encourage one another.

Set a Budget

I get asked often how we budget for family night. For us, it is a category in our budget. We allocate a certain amount of money to family night activities every single month. We do not always go out and spend money to do something fun. We like to get creative and try to find fun things we can do that cost little to no money. There are so many fun things to do in your own community, including heading to the library for a free activity or checking out your local parks and recreation office for their calendar of events.

Don't Forget the Treat

At the end of each family night, we love to share a yummy treat. It is something we look forward to each week. Sometimes it is homemade cookies or a cake, and other times it is a box of ice cream sandwiches from the store. We love to end our family night with treats because dishing out a bit of sugary goodness at the end of the night tends to keep those children around for a little bit longer. This is especially beneficial if you have teenagers in your home. Let each family member have a chance to pick a dessert and even help make it. No matter who chooses the dessert, you are sure to have a fun-filled night!

Around the Dinner Table

If your schedule is hectic, like most moms I know, take advantage of dinnertime. Pick a time each day that dinner is served. No one time will work for everyone. Choose a time that works for you and your family. Commit to sitting down as a family, as often as you can, to share a meal. Don't forget to turn off the TV and put down the cell phones. Let your children tell you about their days. Tell them about yours. Take back dinner so you can have more time together, enjoying a yummy meal. Most families that commit to sharing a meal together each day are stronger and eat out a whole lot less. Since dinner is something you know you will be planning each day, you will be more likely to take care in what you are cooking. Keep it simple and healthy. And don't forget fun!

If dinner is a hard time for you, pick another meal. Try breakfast or lunch. Just pick a meal and share it together. You will be surprised at how talkative you all will get while sharing a delicious feast. In our home, some of our best laughs happen around the kitchen table. This is when stories are shared and giggles are had.

You have the creative power of making it work for you. Look at your family's schedule and see what days you can plan to have everyone eat a meal together. The more effort you put into it, the more you will get out of it. Have a family meeting to express your need for a family meal. Let your family know how important it is to sit down often throughout the week. The more that everyone is on the same page, the more likely it is that everyone will make the time to come together.

Try and Try Again

Hubby and I joke a lot about the fact that I do not have a green thumb. I don't even have a green pinkie. It's that bad! I have always had a big dream of a lush garden in my front yard. I dream of vines cascading the side of my home and freshly bloomed flowers surrounding it. Sounds beautiful, right? That husband of mine even built me some planter boxes from old reclaimed wood to grow my lush garden in. Each year, I plant my seeds and give them a good watering. After a few weeks, something wondrous happens. Little sprouts begin to form. This is when I get all giddy and do a little end-zone dance in my front yard. I start to get the feeling that my thumbs are turning green, and then it happens. The complete letdown. My seedlings stop growing. I am never sure what happens to prevent my plants from continuing to grow. It could be that my soil is poor or it gets too hot. It could also be the fact that life gets busy, and I sometimes forget to go outside and water my little garden. Even though this happens quite often to my seedlings—far more than I care to admit—I am always hopeful that maybe this time I will channel that mama who has a green thumb. Although I usually end up with a less-than-inspiring garden, I still keep trying. What can I say? I am tenacious!

Just like I keep trying to become that gardener I know is hiding somewhere inside me (*deep* inside me), it is important to consistently try to have family night. Some weeks you may completely forget (I have done that a time or two), or maybe it doesn't turn out the way you'd plan. In the words of my Italian grandfather, "Forget about it!" Dust yourself off. Try again.

Five Tips to Having a Successful Family Night

1. *Have a good attitude.* Whether you've had a bad day, you're feeling a bad case of the grumps coming on, or you are just in a plain old pouty mood, you need to have a good attitude. Nothing is a bigger family night mood killer than someone with a stinky attitude.

2. *Sharing is caring.* Let anyone who wants to get a chance to plan a fun activity. Let your kids be included in the planning of family night activities. It truly makes a difference when children get to have their little voices heard. It lets them know that their opinions matter and that they too can have amazing ideas.

3. *Make it a priority.* Make it something that everyone participates in. If you make it a priority, then your children will too. Set a day each week when family night occurs. For us, it is usually Mondays. Having a day set aside each week, makes us accountable. It also gives us something to look forward to each week!

4. *Set aside your expectations.* Family night does not have to be something that costs a lot and is extravagant. It is not about the money spent, but rather the time spent together. Set aside your expectations and just have fun. Sometimes our family nights end in little redhead wrestling matches, with Mom and Dad heaving big heavy sighs, and that's okay. We are sticking to our Monday night routine. We do this because no matter how crazy our house can get, we know that any time spent together is time well spent.

5. *Be flexible.* If you had a hike planned but it rains, don't forego your plans for the night. Do something else. If someone is feeling under the weather, go with a movie night in. If your little ones are excited about trying out a new card game, but you planned to have a homemade pizza night, see if you can combine both ideas. The more that the whole family is included in the planning, the better. Make family night less about who gets to have their way and more about enjoying quality time together.

One Hundred Fun Family Night Activities

Most of these ideas cost little to no money. When an activity comes up that does cost, don't worry. If you budget money for family nights each month, you will have the money to cover it. Check and see what deals are happening around you. A lot of places give discounts for residents and even have free days, so check for those before you start spending money. Again, remember that family night is not about the amount of money you spend, but rather how you spend your time together. Unplug and enjoy time with your family this week.

1. Go geocaching. This is a great way to go on an actually treasure hunt with the family.
2. Camp out in the yard. Don't forget to make s'mores!
3. Visit a local state park and have a picnic.
4. Have a drive-in movie night right in your home. Get some boxes and have your littles design them to look like cars. You can use paper plates for headlights. Once it is movie time, line them up in front of the TV and have the kids sit inside them. Pop in your movie, and you have your own kid-friendly drive-in. Make sure you don't forget the popcorn and snacks!
5. Build a fort in the living room and camp out for the night.

6. Go bowling.
7. If you live near water, head to the beach for a fun family afternoon of playing in the sand.
8. Check out a local museum in your area. Most museums have free days for locals each year.
9. Go on an after-dark treasure hunt. Make a treasure map and then use flashlights to guide you along the way.
10. Go ice-skating.
11. Go to the dollar theater.
12. Play flashlight tag.
13. Try glow-in-the-dark bowling. Fill old soda bottles with water and glow sticks. This makes for a fun night!
14. Head to your local zoo for the afternoon.
15. Go to the park for a game of basketball.
16. Play hide-and-seek in the dark.
17. Play a game of freeze tag.
18. Have a movie marathon. We love to do this around the holidays with Christmas movies!
19. Go for a drive. Don't forget to pack a yummy snack!
20. Go for a hike.
21. Head out on a family bike ride.
22. Have a pajama movie night.
23. Have a bake-off challenge. Boys versus girls!
24. Enjoy a pizza night.
25. Go out for ice cream or have an ice cream bar at home.
26. If you have a fire pit, roast marshmallows.
27. Head to a playground you've never been to before.
28. Hold some Family Olympics. Set up a bunch of games and compete. Don't forget to make some fun aluminum foil medals!
29. Play minute-to-win-it games.
30. Grab some blankets and head outside to watch the stars. If you have a telescope, bring that along too!
31. Volunteer at an animal shelter together.
32. Play hopscotch.
33. Take family photos. Get out the camera and have some fun taking photos of each other.
34. Make some sock puppets. Gather your old socks, decorate them, and then put on a show!
35. Spend the night looking at old photo albums and telling stories.
36. Watch old family videos.
37. Go roller-skating.
38. Paint on canvas together.
39. Put a puzzle together.
40. Play a card game.

41. Check a dance DVD out from the library and learn a new dance.

42. Have a formal family dinner. Set the table with your best tableware and have everyone dress up. Don't forget to use your best manners!

43. Go on a walk around the neighborhood.

44. Scatter sunshine to your neighbors. Place bottle of SunnyD on your neighbors' doorsteps and leave a little note. You never know whose day you will make a bit more sunny!

45. Play "Name That Tune."

46. Play mini-golf.

47. Play a board game.

48. Heart attack someone on your street. Leave paper hearts all over their door and porch. Don't forget to leave a sweet treat. This is a great way to let people know you are thinking of them!

49. Make your own bubble solution out of dish soap and water. Add glycerin, if you have it, for firmer bubbles. Go outside, blow bubbles, and have fun!

50. Paint your own mug. Buy inexpensive glass mugs and acrylic paint and have each family member decorate a mug for his or her own use.

51. Cook a meal that everyone agrees on. Let the whole family help in preparing it!

52. Make a family movie. Write up a script together, put together some costumes, and film it!

53. Make a family cookbook.

54. Build a birdhouse together.

55. Plant a garden.

56. Do some genealogy work. Work on a family genealogy chart together. Talk about distant relatives and family history.

57. Set up an obstacle course in your backyard. Use things like hula hoops and jump ropes to create an outdoor obstacle course in which you can compete with each other for best time.

58. Create a family newsletter to send out to your family and friends.

59. Paint and decorate the family mailbox.

60. Make a craft together.

61. Create a fun piece of art for your home together.

62. Go to a free movie in the park.

63. Go to a free music concert in your community.

64. Go swimming.

65. Turn the sprinklers on and run through them.

66. Jump on the trampoline.

67. Have a LEGO night. Pull

out all your blocks and build together.

68. Have a paper airplane competition.
69. Start a thankful jar.
70. Make some knitted hats for charity.
71. Create a karaoke night.
72. Go to a local high school and see a stage production or performance.
73. Listen to a book on tape.
74. Go to the library to check out books.
75. Play Chubby Bunny with marshmallows. See how many you can stuff in our mouth while still saying "chubby bunny."
76. Play charades.
77. Play Pictionary.
78. Play hangman.
79. Read a book together.
80. Play tennis.
81. Play a game of dominoes.
82. Enjoy an ice cream sundae bar at home.
83. Make Playdough.
84. Have a living room dance party. Take turns being the DJ and have fun dancing!
85. Play a game of telephone.
86. Go to a downtown art festival.
87. Enjoy a holiday parade with your kids.
88. Compete in a local 5k together.

89. Make cards to send to family and friends.
90. Play video games together.
91. Have a *Just Dance* competition.
92. Have a pillow fight.
93. Fly a kite.
94. Play paintball.
95. Go to the batting cages.
96. Play laser tag.
97. Have a fondue night at home.
98. Watch a documentary.
99. Have a Nerf gun fight.
100. Play balloon volleyball.

Chapter 9

Celebrating on
a Budget

In this chapter, I talk a lot about Christmas. My family uses the same financial planning tools throughout the rest of the year that we use for Christmas. These are tried-and-true strategies, so you can use them to enjoy the holidays and stay out of debt as well. As you read through these pages, like with everything else in this book, see what few things you can do right now to save your family money. Living frugally is not about taking the fun out of life; it is about putting it back in. When we live frugally and we are smart with our money, we are able to enjoy life more because we are not bogged down by financial stress. Remember this key fact as you read this chapter and the chapters that follow. Life is a beautiful thing and is meant to be enjoyed.

The holidays can be a time of great joy, with family gatherings and fun, but they can also be a time of great stress and debt. Instead of putting money aside beforehand, many people go shopping with their plastic cards, not thinking of what they are spending or how they will ultimately pay for those brightly wrapped gifts under the tree. I was recently reading an article from CNBC *News*. It said that "many Americans are still entering the holiday season unprepared to cope with the expenses that crop up around this time of year." It also said that, for some people, "the holiday season brings so much financial pressure, they would prefer to skip it altogether."[1] Isn't that sad? The holidays are meant to be enjoyed, not dreaded!

Hubby and I have been married for over ten years, so we have spent a lot of time celebrating together. It's one of our favorite things to do. Just like with everything in our budgeting life, we didn't start off celebrating on a budget. We started out like many of you probably have. We would make a list of whom we had to buy for, and then we would go shopping, probably spending way too much. We didn't have a game plan, a budget, or any clue about what we were doing. We would justify that it was Christmas or so and so's birthday, and you had to spend money for those special occasions. We stayed in this practice for many years. Then that wonderful day happened when we decided to change our financial situation. I knew that living a budgeted life needed to apply to everything, including holidays and birthdays. Budgeting every day of the year only to forget it come holiday time would not help my family. If I was going to change the way I was shopping and spending, I had to do it in every facet of my life. That had to include the holidays.

Hubby and I both grew up celebrating differently. In my family, when we celebrated birthdays, we were a bit extravagant. The birthday person would get to pick out their favorite restaurant, and we would all go out to eat. We would then come home, open presents, and enjoy a store-bought cake. We also had a birthday party, where we could invite friends over to swim and BBQ. I remember having a birthday party at Chuck E. Cheese's. That was a pretty fun birthday of pizza and arcade games. My five-year-old self rocked at Skee-Ball! Birthdays were always a special day, spent in the company of family and friends. Hubby's family was not as extravagant. He comes from a military family of six. He also shares his birthday with his twin brother. When he was younger, his mother would make themed cakes for her children from scratch. There are many pictures of fancy cakes, with little children gathered around smiling. I love these pictures! After cake, my hubby's family would have a small celebration at home with a few small gifts. Birthdays were much more low-key. They were still just as special, but they didn't spend a lot of money. His parents were supporting a large family on a small income. Hubby learned the need for frugality at a young age.

I recently asked him what he remembered about growing up and celebrating the holidays with his family. He said that he remembered a lot of group gifts (gifts that his family could use together). He also remembered going "people watching" with his dad. He said that it was something that he enjoyed doing with his dad year-round. My family was more lavish with gifts and parties. His family moved a lot because his father was a Marine. A lot of the time, they lived away from family, so their celebrating consisted of their immediate family and friends from whatever city they were living in at the time. Our different childhood experiences have shaped how we view holidays and birthdays. When Hubby and I got married, we both had some different birthday and holiday experiences that we were bringing to the table. We had to figure out a way to mesh those together so we could create our own fun traditions.

Hubby and I were married in November, which meant that Christmas was just around the corner. That first Christmas, we set a budget for each other in regards to Christmas gift giving. Once the budget was set, we went shopping for one another. I have always been a crafter, so Hubby went to the dollar store to find me some goodies to craft with. He only had so much to spend, so he got creative with what he bought. I was a bit different. To me, a budget was only a suggestion. I didn't know you were actually supposed to stay within that limit (*oh, my naive self*). When gift giving time came, there was a definite different in the gifts. Hubby followed the rules. I on the other hand, did my own thing. This pattern would follow for the next few years. Rather than setting a budget, I would simply make a list of whom I had to buy for and go shopping. I would be deep in the "happy holiday" mood. I would be so focused on this, I wouldn't think about how we were going to pay things off after Santa was gone and we were greeting a new year.

Over time, I learned how to celebrate without using my credit card or sending my bank account into the negative. I learned how to enjoy birthdays and holidays without feeling like we were broke the rest of the month. By budgeting and setting money aside for these celebratory times, having a frugal mind-set, and being a strategic shopper, I was able to learn how to shop smart, stick to a budget, and enjoy holidays without the stress of overspending.

The span of time between my son's birthday in October and my daughter's birthday in January is my favorite time of the year. With two birthdays, our wedding anniversary, and all the holidays in between, I am sure you can see how that time of year can be quite a budget buster in our home. Between family parties, food, holiday gifts, birthday gifts, holiday outings, and all that good stuff, it is easy to feel overwhelmed and broke before the holiday fun even begins. I don't know about you, but I don't like spending my time stressed about how we will pay for everything. I want to spend it enjoying being with family and friends. Since a grumpy mama is no good any time of year, I follow a few simple rules to help my family have a great time and stay within our budget as well.

Set a Budget

First things first: anytime you are planning to spend money, you need to set a budget. If you don't have a budget, then you don't have a plan. Remember, we talked about this previously? It applies to basically everything. Having a plan is a good thing and not having a plan is not.

Each holiday season, Hubby and I sit down and decide how much we can spend on Christmas. Whether our year went well and we were able to save very much through the year will determine how much we can spend on Christmas. Throughout the year, we try to save a little bit each month to our holidays account. We use this money saved to pay for Easter baskets in April, Halloween costumes in October, and Christmas presents in December. By saving throughout the year, we take a lot of stress out of the holidays.

To find out what your family should budget for the holidays, look at last year's spending. This will help you get a better idea of what you have spent in the past. Once you know what you spent last year, you can realistically set a budget for the upcoming year. If what you spent last year is more than you can afford to set aside throughout the year, then maybe you need to cut back on Christmas spending. Your friends and relatives don't want you to go into debt for the holidays. They just want to spend time with you. Setting a Christmas shopping budget does not mean you love your family less. Money does not equate to love. Never forget this.

Sit down with your spouse and actually talk about what you are going to spend on Christmas. Be specific. So many people forget to do this. They shop and spend, and then after Christmas they are shocked at how much they spent. Everyone's budget will be different. Pick one that fits into your current financial situation. Look at how much you have saved throughout the year and how much you can "save" in December to go toward

"Our get-togethers usually are with family. We all potluck. That relieves one family of the burden of the cost and preparation of a meal for twenty-plus people. Even the guys that don't cook will volunteer to bring plates and utensils."

—Regina

"For DIY gifts, you can create coupons for family and friends. I make the kids a coupon book for their stockings. Each one says something different that they can turn in. 'Stay up fifteen minutes later,' 'manicure from Mom,' 'dinner of your choice.' For friends, why not include some like 'dinner at our house' or 'free night of babysitting.'"

—Aly

Christmas gifts. When Hubby and I sit down to budget, we decide how much we will spend on our children first. Stocking stuffers are included in this budget. We then decide how much we will spend on each other and on our other family members. When money has been extra tight at the holidays, we forego the presents for each other. Sometimes we will wait till we get our tax returns and shop for each other then. We always make sure that we have money for the kids first.

When we shop, I go with my Christmas list in hand. I also bring along my calculator. I input each item so I know that we are staying within the budget. If one of the children has asked for something more expensive, they may only get a few things.

When we shop for the children, we make a night out of it. It is one of my favorite dates of the year. We ask the grandparents to watch the kids, and we go out together with Christmas lists in hand. We laugh and talk as we go through the aisles of toys and children's goodies. After our shopping is done, we get something to eat. Usually, it is a simple meal. A budgeted run through the drive-through is all this mama needs to have a happy date with her hubby. I look forward to this outing every year, when it's just a night to goof around with my hubby and shop for those goodies my sweet littles will open up on Christmas morning.

When buying presents for other family members, there are a few things we do. First, we set a price limit for each person. We usually have a ten-dollar limit. This limit is the same when birthdays come around as well. This is a reasonable amount for us because we have a pretty large extended family. We also do Secret Santa with my hubby's family. This helps a ton! Everyone picks a name out of a hat. We set a ten-dollar limit and then exchange presents at a family Christmas Eve brunch. This is such an amazing help to our family. Instead of spending, say, $150 on presents for my in-laws, we only spend $40. It also takes stress off of the shopper. I am able to spend more time relaxing during the Christmas season than figuring out what to buy for my family. I love them to pieces, but sometimes all that shopping and spending can wear a person out, not to mention my checkbook.

Pay Cash

It's a basic concept, right? We do this throughout the year when we pay for groceries and toiletries, so why not do it during the holidays as well? Our rule is if we have to charge it, then we don't need it. Yes, there are exceptions, but this is a good one to follow as a general rule. Credit cards are for emergencies only. Where Christmas is concerned, we only use cash. Going through with my calculator makes me accountable to my budget. I try to remember that if I go over budget, it means money taken away from our bills being paid or groceries being bought. Also, having cash means once the money is gone, I have no more money for Christmas shopping. It helps keep my shopaholic tendencies at bay.

Go Homemade or Thrifted

Whenever I can, I go homemade. This is a great way to save money. I always try to find projects where I have most of the items already in my craft stash. If I have to purchase anything to make a present, I always go to thrift stores first. One year, I made rag tie wreaths for my sisters-in-law. I bought sheets at a thrift store to make them. This saved me tons in the fabric department. Another year, I made Little Miss a beauty salon set with faux make-up. I took old curling irons and stuff I wasn't using. I cut off the cords and made a beautician apron and a hair salon cape for her doll out of fabric I already had. It was a simple thing to make and provided many hours of fun for my redheaded princess.

I also love to look for gifts at thrift stores. There are so many wonderful things donated to thrift stores. Most stores save all their Christmas decor and stuff for December. This is great, because you can always give Christmas decorations as a gift or incorporate it into planned crafts you have. Look at the toys and clothes sections too. You never know what gems you may find. I have found so many great items that have made perfect gifts for friends and family.

When making presents for grandparents, I try to go the sentimental and homemade route. My parents love pictures of their grandkids. Every year, I make a calendar and order it from Costco. My mom looks forward to this present each year. I used to order from another online photography site, but I realized that I could save myself ten dollars by going through Costco. Make sure that when you go homemade and need to print something, you compare prices. Doing this and taking advantage of deals and coupons will save you tons!

Shop around

Shopping around is not just for groceries. It is for anytime you are going to buy something. Shopping smart will save you money. Just because your budget allows you to spend ten dollars per person does not mean you have to spend all of it. If you find a great deal, then you can save that extra money. This money can then be used for other things. There are so many deal-of-the-day sites on the web. Some of my favorites are *My Cents of Style, Paparazzi Accessories,* and *GroopDealz.* Last year, I purchased presents for my sisters-in-law, who all have birthdays in December and January, from these sites. I was able to buy gifts for three people and only spend sixteen dollars. I budgeted thirty dollars, but I was able to find some great deals. All of these sites send me emails when they have deals. I wait for a really good one and plan ahead.

Money can be wasted on toys our kids won't even play with. Kids are bombarded with toy commercials and ads. They are lead to believe that every toy will be amazing. This is not always the case. I can't even believe how much money we wasted when we first had my son. He would think everything was cool and that he *had* to have it. We would buy it and then find out that it wasn't really something he would play with. It was just something that looked cool on TV. Now we only buy things we know our children will play with. Before birthdays and Christmas, we take them to the store to browse the aisles. We let them go up and down the toy aisles to check out all the goodies. We watch what they gravitate toward. We then think about how our children play. My son is not into dress-up things, but my daughter is. He will see Spider-Man masks and lightsabers and swear he will play with them every day. We know from experience now that he won't. He hates dressing up. This would be one of those things we would not buy, even if he asked for it. Shopping smart is a great way to only buy what your children will actually use. We have a limited budget. I want to get as much bang for my buck as possible. I want to make sure my kids will truly enjoy everything they get from us.

Another way to shop smart is to price match. A lot of stores will price match competitors' prices during the holidays. You bring in your ad and show them the cheaper price. They then will honor that price. Ask your local toy store or department store to see if they price match. It never hurts to ask. Some stores even have layaway programs. This is a great way to get presents and not charge them to a credit card. You pick out your items and then bring them to customer service. They then put them all on hold for you. You make payments throughout the month of December. This is great for people who get paid by the week or who are shopping with a

Christmas bonus. Check out your local store to see what options would suit your family's needs and budget.

Black Friday—the Good and the Bad

You can also take advantage of the great sales that happen come Tur-key-time. I am talking about Black Friday. It is the biggest shopping day of the year, where men and women get up early or don't even sleep at all so they can take advantage of stellar deals. I used to be one of those mamas, waiting in line at four in the morning with my circulars in hand. I scored a lot of great deals this way, like that Disney Princess doll for five bucks or that chevron-patterned hair straighter for ten dollars. Yes, I scored some amazing, out-of-this-world deals, but I also bought a lot of things I didn't really need. I was like many consumers, getting excited over rock-bottom prices on new goodies such as electronics, children's toys, computers, clothes, and more. Although the prices were amazing, I was purchasing things I didn't need. I would get caught up in the experience of Black Friday.

If you are one of those people who loves to shop on this consumer-driven day, be smart and be wary. Make sure that you are following some type of plan or budget. Don't buy stuff just because it is a good deal. Never forget that it is not a good deal if you don't really need it. Look at the ads before you shop and ask yourself, "Do I really need this?" Those circulars can be oh so tempting! They offer deals on almost anything you could think of. Even the most practical of shoppers can fall prey to an impulse-purchase or two among the sea of doorbusters, circulars, and crowded lines. With the chance for temptation running high, it is easy for shoppers to spend over their budgeted amounts. Ask yourself, "Would I buy this item normally?" Regardless of how much the price was slashed, if the item is something you don't need or are only going to use a handful of times, it is more than likely a waste of money for you to buy. Make a list of what you intend to buy and stick to it. Go through the store with blinders so you focus on the items you need and ignore those deals that can send you over your budget in no time. When you make a budget, bring it in cash. Doing this will prevent you from overspending. Tell yourself that once the cash is gone, your shopping ends. If you are someone who loves to shop with a buddy, go with a buddy who will help support you in your plan not to overspend. Make sure that you are an encouraging shopping buddy as well.

Quality, Not Quantity

My children may not have a truckload of toys under the tree, but what they do have will last. It is easy to see toys in catalogs and say, "What a great price!" I am wary of this because we have done this before and the toys have not lasted. My son is pretty hard on toys, so we always look for something that will last. It is not worth it to buy a lot of cheaply made items just so you have a huge amount of gifts under the tree. Buy items for your family that will last and stand up to wear and tear. Be conscious of all purchases. Whether you are buying thrifted items or brand-new items, think of each purchase as an investment. Make sure you get the most bang for your buck where quality and price are concerned.

Host a Potluck-Style Party

Hosting big holiday parties can be so much fun, but along with them, you can create a food budget that begins to skyrocket before you even step foot inside a grocery store. Because of this, our family likes to do the holidays (and any other family get-together) potluck style. The person hosting provides the main dish, while everyone else brings side dishes and desserts. This is a great way to enjoy each other's company and not break the bank.

I have a friend who takes it a step further. Each year, she throws an after-Thanksgiving leftovers party. She invites a few close friends over the day after Thanksgiving, and they all share a yummy meal together. The great thing about this type of party is that it's a no-stress kind of event. The party requires no extra prep. The only requirement is to bring whatever you didn't eat the day before. Think outside the box, and remember to have fun with family gatherings. By being creative, you can still host a party without draining your wallet.

Make Your Own Decor

I am a crafty gal. Making holiday decor is one thing I look forward to each year. I love pulling out my past creations and thinking about what new item I would like to add to my collection. Pinterest is a great way to find inspiration. There are so many project ideas out there! You can find simple projects to make with what you already have on hand. Don't forget to get those little hands involved as well! We always love making paper chains and handprint turkeys each year. Having your children take part in

114

the decorating not only provides a frugal way to decorate, but it also makes their eyes light up when they see their masterpieces on display for all to see.

Rethink Expensive Traditions and Make New Ones

Are there certain traditions that you maintain out of obligation and not interest? It may be something we did as kids, but as we have grown and started families of our own, we may feel like that tradition does not hold the same meaning—especially if it is an expensive one. Early in my marriage, Hubby and I use to always visit this park in town when December came around. This park would be decked out in all its Christmas glory. Different companies would come and set up amazing Christmas displays. It was absolutely breathtaking. We did this for many years, but over time, we realized that we didn't always look forward to it the way we did other family traditions. Without knowing it, we were making ourselves follow this crazy tradition we made up, year after year, even though we didn't really want to go anymore. It was really expensive and quite a drive for us. One Christmas, Hubby and I decided that this tradition was one we would leave in the past. If you have a similar tradition, don't be afraid to change it. There is no foul in making new traditions and changing old ones if they don't work for your family anymore. There are plenty of other ways to enjoy being together as a family.

One of my favorite traditions is from when I was a child myself. When I was growing up, setting up the tree was always a family affair. We would put on Christmas music, and everyone would gather around the tree and talk about the different ornaments and where they came from. Each year, my mom and dad would give us special ornaments. I always looked forward to those special ornaments in my stocking. My favorite was the ceramic ballerina. It was perfect, since I had started learning pointe that year. I now hang this ornament on my own tree. I loved this tradition so much, I wanted to carry it on when I got married. In the beginning, Hubby and I would exchange ornaments for stocking stuffers. He has always gotten me ceramic cows. I have a thing for cows. They are just too gosh-darn cute! I would get him bulldogs and ornaments that often shared an inside joke between the two of us. As children came along, we had them join in the tradition. Over time, buying four ornaments became a bit much, so Hubby and I decided to keep the tradition, but changed it a bit to suit our family's budget. We now only do ornaments for the kids and a family ornament to add to our tree each year.

> *Moving items around your house can breathe new life into them. This is particularly true during the holiday season. Do a bit of rearranging to get into the holiday spirit!*

As we take out each ornament, little hands grasp the delicate bobbles. Questions of where the balls come from arise. I love to tell stories about the ornament we got when Daddy was in Iraq. We bought a "Support the Troops" ornament so we would never forget that time in our lives. It was a trying time, but one we got through as a family. We have a metal lizard from when Hubby and I went to the Grand Canyon. We tell the kids about their first Christmases and each one that followed. Hubby usually throws in a few tall tales as well. It is a time I look forward to each year.

Consider what traditions are important to you, and explore the idea of starting your own new traditions. Do you buy a real tree because you feel you should but secretly hate the falling pine needles? Do you prepare a turkey but secretly want to prepare something different? New traditions can breathe new life into your regular family gatherings. Get together as a family and decide what you want to try out this year. As long as you are doing it as a family, you can't go wrong!

Birthdays

We follow similar steps for celebrating our family's birthdays on a budget as we do the holidays. We always set a budget, and it typically stays the same each year. We do this so we can put a bit of money aside each month. We typically spend fifty dollars on a gift and fifty dollars on an outing or party (the kids get to choose). It ends up totaling one hundred dollars each year. Since we have two kids, we know we have to save two hundred dollars into our birthday account throughout the year to cover birthday celebrations. Each month, we contribute seventeen dollars into our "birthday" account. By saving all year, we are prepared when birthdays roll around. We let them pick a fun outing or they can have a birthday party. It is up to them. Sometimes they choose to have a themed party. When that happens, they know we have fifty dollars to spend on it. If they choose a fun outing, as our son did one year when he chose Go-Karts, we spent twenty-five dollars on Go-Karts and twenty-five dollars going out to lunch. By sticking to a budget, we could go out as a family without breaking the bank. When the children are thinking about what they want for their birthdays, they know that Mom and Dad spend fifty

dollars. They make a little wish list, and then I try to get the best deal
I can. A lot of times when video games are asked for, I look on Ebay
to find a deal. Quite often I am able to find one. I always compare the
prices between Ebay, Wal-Mart, Target, and Amazon. If you are ordering
online, be sure to include shipping in the total price.

Date Night

I couldn't end this chapter without sharing some fun ideas for that
date night with your love. For us, date nights are important. It is a time
for you and your spouse to reconnect after a long week. It is a time to
refuel the fires of romance. Remember that feeling you had when you first
started dating? I still remember those butterflies I would get and the way
his green eyes would light up when he laughed (they still do that). I love
those little moments we shared as we learned more about each other and
fell in love. When you date your spouse, you are reminded that they are
your favorite person in the world and that they are truly your best friend.
Even after more than ten years, I am still learning new things about my
husband. Oh, and I still sometimes get butterflies when he walks into the
room. He knows me better than anyone else in this world—just like how
I know him best. Choosing to date your spouse allows those feelings of
love, friendship, and passion to never go away. Also, the more you date
your spouse, the closer you will become. As you go throughout this life,
change is inevitable. If you are constantly talking, listening, and sharing
with one another, you will grow together and not apart.

I love to think of marriage as being a little plant. We all know that
a plant needs soil, water, and sunshine to thrive. If it doesn't have those
things, it starts to wither and die. For my husband and I, our faith in
the Lord is our soil. It keeps us firmly planted. This is similar to how a
plant needs soil to keep it strong and firm. Just as we give plants water
and sunshine to grow, we need to nurture our own marriages with water
and sunshine. We must take time from each day to talk and listen to
one another.

Whether it is when you are making dinner for the family or after you
put the kids to bed, it is important to have time together. Remember that
before kids came along, it was just the two of you. Someday your munchkins will grow up. They will have families of their own. If you make your
world completely about those sweet munchkins, you may be shocked by
who is sitting next to you when all the chickadees leave the nest.

Make each other a priority. I remember when my husband first shared his priority list with me. We had gone for a drive and were sitting in my parents' driveway talking (we were engaged at the time). I asked him if I was his number one priority. Let's just say I was a bit shocked when he said I wasn't. I was so confused. This was the man I was going to marry, and I was not his number one priority? What the heck?! He could see my face drop and quickly replied, "You're number two." Yeah, like that made it better, hot shot! Then he finished his thought, and I think I fell in love with him a little bit deeper. He told me that his priorities would always be, first the Lord, second his wife, and third his children. I mean, how could I argue with that list? He has stuck to these priorities since that day, and I am so thankful for that. Make your spouse a top priority and your marriage will thrive.

There are so many fun things you can do as a couple. I have compiled a list to help get you started. Whether it is an evening spent on the couch watching a movie or going out for a quick bite to eat, we spend time together. Compromise so that each person gets to do a date they like now and then. Dating your spouse does not have to cost a fortune. Just set a budget and enjoy that time together!

One Hundred Date-Night Ideas for the Year

Fall

1. Hop in the car and go for a drive. Check out the scenery and listen to some of your favorite songs.
2. Rake piles of leaves to jump in. This isn't just for kids and puppy dogs. You and your love can have fun acting like little kids yourselves.
3. Host a couples' Halloween party.
4. Check out what history reenactments are going on in your area. These are usually free or fairly inexpensive to watch.
5. Jump in the car and check out some model homes. It is such a fun way to dream with your spouse and get some great decorating ideas!
6. Set up an empty inflatable swimming pool with blankets, some yummy snacks, and hot chocolate outside. Snuggle with your love and check out the night sky.
7. Take advantage of the fall festivities around you (hay rides, corn mazes, and yummy apple cider).
8. Get into the kitchen and try out a new recipe together. Cooking as a team is always fun!

9. Take a community education class together.

10. If you're into photography, spend the day walking around a nearby town or city. Trade the camera back and forth to see who comes out with the best shots. This would be absolutely beautiful in the fall and spring!

11. Enjoy a seasonal activity like pumpkin carving, making hot chocolate from scratch, grilling outside, and so on.

12. Go apple picking at your local orchard.

13. Create a time capsule. Write notes to each other. Add pictures and other goodies to it. Plan to open it up in five or ten years.

14. See an improv show.

15. Go to the movies.

16. Throw your own prom for you and some friends. Ask your partner to the dance in a creative way.

17. Play *Just Dance.*

18. Go horseback riding.

19. Have a fall couple photography session.

20. Challenge each other to a Wii tournament.

21. Watch the sunset.

22. Make a dessert together.

23. Watch airplanes take off or land.

Winter

24. Make your favorite warm treat and go for a drive to check out all the holiday lights in your neighborhood.

25. Go Christmas shopping together.

26. Go pick out a Christmas tree.

27. Go ice-skating.

28. Make finger foods and sit in front of the fire. Have an indoor picnic.

29. Plan a fondue night with friends.

30. Have a snowball fight.

31. Go sledding.

32. Test-drive a car just for fun.

33. Go to the indoor pool and swim.

34. Get Grandma or Grandpa to watch the kids and enjoy a quiet dinner at home.

35. If you have a fire pit, roast marshmallows.

36. Act like a tourist. When you've lived somewhere for a long time, you tend to forget what drives people there to visit in the first place. Dedicate an afternoon to checking out landmarks in your area.

37. Volunteer together.

38. Check out a high school or college show production. These are always inexpensive and are a great way

to support your local community.

39. Invite friends over for a game of charades.

40. Have a Christmas movie marathon night.

41. Invite friends over to make gingerbread houses.

42. Plan a group date of caroling and sweet treats.

43. Create an at-home spa experience.

44. Bake cookies together.

Spring

45. Go bird watching.

46. Learn to play pool.

47. Plan a game night for you and a group of friends. Don't forget the yummy snacks too!

48. Meet at a park and have a lunch picnic.

49. If you have gardens in your area, go for a walk and hold hands while checking out all the new blooms.

50. Go for a hike.

51. Go for a bike ride.

52. Try a new exercise class together.

53. Go on a walk around the park.

54. Check out your local zoo or aquarium.

55. Go out for ice cream.

56. Play a game.

57. Go bowling.

58. Go roller-skating.

59. Check out a local museum.

60. Try out karaoke.

61. Go out for smoothies or coffee.

62. Try out a brand-new restaurant.

63. Cheer on an amateur sports team in your town. It's just as fun as supporting a professional team, but tickets are so much cheaper!

64. Play mini-golf.

65. Plant a garden.

66. Go to a park and feed the ducks.

67. Go fly kites.

68. Visit a farmers' market.

69. Go to the shooting range.

70. Go dancing.

71. Rent a bicycle built for two.

72. Sit on a dock and watch the boats.

73. Go fishing.

74. Jump on the trampoline.

75. Have a minute-to-win-it game night.

Summer

76. Head to the mall for a bit of window-shopping. You can always end the night with a yummy treat from the food court.

77. Plan a progressive dinner with friends! Everyone dresses up, and different courses of the meal are eaten

at different people's houses.

78. Sneak off to the library together. Have fun checking out some new books and enjoying the quiet time together.

79. Try out a new hobby together, like painting, cooking, or ceramics.

80. Have a movie night at home. Pop some popcorn and snuggle on the couch, watching a favorite flick.

81. Have an old-fashioned campout in the living room. Feel free to make a tent out of blankets too!

82. Lay out under the stars and check for constellations.

83. Hit a bucket of balls at the driving range.

84. Head to the batting cages.

85. Go to an arcade for a night of fun.

86. Go to a local park and rent a canoe or paddleboards.

87. Play a game of Monopoly through until someone wins. Play music (instead of the TV) in the background. You'll have fun conversations.

88. Go to a flea market or thrift store. You don't have to buy anything. Sometimes it is fun to just look around.

89. Make homemade ice cream.

90. See what free events are available in your area, like art shows, festivals, and music events. You can find this on your city's website.

91. Go to the beach.

92. Most communities have movies in the park. Check out what movies your town is showing and plan a date.

93. Go to a carnival.

94. Go to the drive-in.

95. Have a kid-free slumber party in the living room.

96. Race go-karts.

97. Create a bucket list, and then start doing the items on the list.

98. Visit a food festival.

99. Head to the lake with friends to make a bonfire.

100. Host a couples' BBQ.

Whether you have a lot of money to spend or very little, you can make the celebrations in your life a time to remember. Plan, prepare, budget, and enjoy that family of yours. Our families are a gift. Enjoy every moment you get with them. Think outside the box and get creative.

NOTES

1. Christina Cheddar Berk, "Why One Poll Says 45% Would Rather Skip Christmas," CNBC Consumer Nation, November 19, 2012, http://www.cnbc.com/id/49880517.

Chapter 10

Eating Out on a Budget

Although frugal living is my thing and what I do, I do have moments where I am an exhausted mama and I want a night off. There are some days when making stuff from scratch and sticking to that meal plan can seem like an absolute bore. Sometimes I want to be a rebel. Sometimes I even—dare I say it—want to eat out. I have nights where all I want to do is dine out on a cheeseburger that I didn't have to make myself. We all have these moments, right? Some may have them more often than others. When those moments arise, don't beat yourself up over it. That is no fun for anyone.

When I first started frugal living, I thought that eating out had to be completely off limits. I had convinced myself that I was only being a good little frugal mama if I always had meals prepared at five o'clock and my family never ate out. The problem was that I was creating a perfect storm for a burnt-out mama. Being a mama is tough, and sometimes the last thing I want to do at the end of the day is to stand over a hot oven, cooking dinner. Over time, I have learned a few tricks so that when those times arise, I can give myself a little grace and indulge. Throughout this chapter, you will find many tips and tricks on how to have the night off in the kitchen and enjoy some quality family time eating a meal you didn't have to prepare. Through careful planning, making the most of deals, and being diligent to that budget of yours, you can eat out and not break the bank.

Gearing up for Eating Out

Budget for It

Every once in a while, we all need a night out, right? I mean who doesn't love going to a restaurant, ordering a delicious meal, and not having to cook or clean up afterward? Sounds like heaven right? I think every mama across the nation is nodding her head in agreement right now. Eating out can be a fun experience when you do it wisely. But going out to a restaurant, only to be left with a jaw-dropping bill is fun for no one. Staying within a set budget can prevent you from a panic attack when the bill arrives

The first thing to remember is that eating out is not an every night sort of thing unless you're swimming in money, which I am not. But if you are, can I please come over and swim too? I'm sure the water is nice, and I wouldn't mind diving in. Because most of us have limited discretionary funds, eating out needs to be done on a budget and done wisely. To succeed in doing it wisely, you must first see if your budget has room for it. Eating out is a luxury—one that should be enjoyed only when bills are paid and your banking account is in the black. If you are not in the black, then that means you have *no money* to eat out with. Charging a dining-out session is not wise. Remember that you won't be paying your original total, you will be paying so much more. That interest sneaks up and will cause things to cost so much more than you originally charged.

Eating out at a restaurant can cost about fifteen dollars per person. For a family of four, that bill adds up quickly. A sixty-dollar hit to your budget (add another $10 if anyone drinks soda or alcohol) is hard to recover from.

At the beginning of each month, or whenever you sit down and review your budget, see if you have any room for a night out. If you do, set the money aside. A night out for each of us may look different. Some may prefer a sit-down meal with waiters, while others would like a quick trip down to their local pizzeria. Whatever your night out looks like, decide how much you can reasonably spend on eating out and set that budget. Setting the budget takes the worry out of the eating-out scenario. If you know the money has already been separated for your night off from the kitchen, then you know you have the money to cover not only all the essentials but the fun stuff too.

Each month, Hubby and I allocate a certain amount of money for eating out. Once this money is gone, we do *not* eat out. You can't spend money you don't have. Some months, our eating-out budget is smaller than others. We base this off whatever else is going on that month. Sit down with your spouse and decide how much you would like to spend. When Hubby and I have a special occasion in mind, like a celebratory dinner, then we will save up our eating-out money for a few months. This enables us to really splurge when celebrating time comes around. No matter how you eat out, set that budget.

Plan

The next thing you should do to gear up for eating out is plan where and when you will be going. These two things can greatly affect how far your eating-out budget stretches. Some restaurants have certain nights when children eat free. Find out what restaurants in your area offer this and what days. By going on a kids-eat-free night, you can save your family at least ten dollars—or even more if you have more kiddos.

Pick a restaurant that is reasonably priced and fits within your budget. If you only have twenty-five dollars to spend on eating out in a month, going to a sit-down restaurant may not be the best option. Find a restaurant you can reasonably afford and enjoy as a family. You can get just as full in a reasonably-priced restaurant on quality food with friendly service. If you're a big eater, an all-you-can-eat buffet may be right for you.

Pick a time of day that suits your schedule and your wallet. Going out to eat for breakfast or lunch usually costs less than dinner but is just as fun. Going out for brunch with the family may be a nice alternative to Friday night dinner, because the restaurants will be less crowded, and everyone will have fun eating something other than cereal and milk.

Menu

In this day and age of astounding technology, there isn't much you can't find on the Internet. This includes menus for all of your favorite restaurants. Having access to the menu before you go to the restaurant is a great way to plan what you will budget for your night out. Nothing is worse than getting to a restaurant only to realize that it is way out of your budget. Go through the different meal options so you have an idea of what you will want to order. Go through with a calculator so you know if the items you are thinking of picking out will fit into whatever budget you have set for the night. I know some may be thinking, *Why do all that work? It takes the fun out of my night out.* Eating out this way does take a bit more prep work, but the benefits far outweigh the work.

Hubby and I rarely go out to a sit-down restaurant, but every once in while, we decide to splurge and go for it! We set a budget and go for a night out together. Hubby loves to look up menus beforehand because it gives us a better idea of the price and type of food that is served at a particular restaurant. Recently, we went to a Japanese restaurant where they cooked the food in front of us. It was amazing! Truly dinner and a show! These types of restaurants are wonderful but can get pretty pricey. We looked up the menu beforehand so we would know what we wanted and how much it would cost. Because we were prepared, there was no surprise when the check came. We knew we had money to cover not only the food but the tip as well.

Make It Special

Make eating out special. With anything in life, the less frequently we do something, the more special it will become. If you have pizza delivery on your speed dial and the delivery guy knows you by name, I would say that eating out has become your fallback instead of something special you do. When you eat out, make it something special you do as a couple or as a family. When you do it less frequently, you will notice that everyone appreciates it a whole lot more.

Money-Saving Tips for Eating out

Now that you know how to plan ahead and budget for eating out, I have a few more money-saving tips to share. These are all things that my own family does to make our eating-out budget stretch.

Don't forget to use coupons. A lot of restaurants send out coupons in the mail. Plan your eating out budget, and then use coupons to make it stretch further!

When special celebrations come up, enjoy it and splurge a little. Saving up for these special occasions in advance means you can splurge but not veer away from your budget.

Shop around and see which local restaurant is offering the best deal. This will save you money and will allow you to get the most bang for your buck!

Whenever we have loose change, we put it in our piggy bank. Once it is full, we cash in our change and go out to eat. It makes for an inexpensive night out.

Use Coupons

Did you know that coupons are not just for grocery shopping? You can find coupons for almost anything. Restaurants often send out coupon fliers in the mail. They usually come with the grocery ads. You can also scan the newspaper for discount coupons, but read the fine print and make sure it's a bargain and not a come-on. Buying an entertainment book that usually offers buy-one-get-one-free coupons can mean real savings for the whole year too!

Don't forget the Internet and the oh-so-fabulous social media. #Itisawesome! The world is becoming more and more tech savvy, which means more ways for companies to get information out to customers. Downloading apps for your favorite restaurants or signing up for mailing lists will put the savings right in your inbox. You can also follow your favorite restaurants via social media. This helps you to stay in the loop for any promotions going on. I do this for quite a few of my favorite food chains. You may be surprised how much you can save.

Eat for Free

Don't you just love that phrase? I do! Some restaurants offer "eat for free" days throughout the year. Whether it is an "eat free on your birthday" deal or a dress-up deal, you can have fun and eat out at the same time. Every year, we dress up as pirates and talk like them too. Why do we do this? To get free doughnuts, of course! This is a promotion that the Krispy Kreme Doughnuts chain does each year during the month of September to celebrate pirates. There is no better way to celebrate being a family than wearing an eye patch and clipping a fake bird onto your shoulder. Oh, and I can't forget the adorable *"Arrrg!"* I hear when people are dressed in full pirate attire. Classic. This type of promotion would be similar to the "dress like a cow day" at Chick-fil-A. We don't have one near us, but I sure do love seeing everyone's cow costumes on Instagram.

Don't forget to call around to your local restaurants and fast food establishments. Many chains will offer days when seniors, kids, or veterans eat free. I am a firm believer of "it doesn't hurt to ask." You never know what money you could be saving if you never ask!

Ditch the Soda and Alcohol Too

Ditching the soda and alcohol is a great way to save while eating out. Most restaurants do not offer free adult drinks with the meal, so that means you are paying an additional three dollars or more for a drink. This can add up fast. Restaurants have a huge profit margin on these drinks. Skip it and your wallet will thank you. Order water instead. Adding a bowl of lemons to go with it will make it a bit more fancy. If you are at a fast food chain, order a water cup rather than bottled water.

Have Dessert at Home

Dessert menus, with huge, tasty close-ups of caloric land mines are on the table for a reason. They are to entice us and have us wanting more. They look so amazing that sometimes we will ignore that stuffed-to-the-gills feeling we already have after dinner. Instead of ordering dessert, try having it at home instead. Pick up a half-gallon of ice cream on the way home from the restaurant or some yummy fruit for a healthier option. That half-gallon of ice cream will give you dessert for the rest of the week for the same price as a single serving at the restaurant.

Say No to Appetizers

I know they always look appetizing (hence the name), but what usually happens? You order some appetizers and spoil your dinner. If an appetizer *is* calling you though, there is a way to satisfy that craving and not overstuff yourself or go over budget. Why not try an appetizer medley as your main dish? This is a great way to try all of those tempting starters and keep your kid syndrome at bay! You could also share the medley with a friend or your spouse to really keep costs down. I always say sharing is caring, and with food it totally applies.

Portions

Here in America, we like things bigger, and because none of us need all of those calories in one sitting, most restaurant portions will actually feed you *and* a friend. Sometimes we have our kids share a meal when we go out if we know that particular restaurant serves huge portions with their kids meals. When we eat at Costco (a great place for an affordable meal), we have our kids share. Their pizza slices are gigantic! You can actually ask to have one slice cut into two. You can do the same with a smoothie and have it served in two cups. Each child gets his or her own plate, but you are only paying for one meal between the two of them! Don't be afraid to ask for an extra plate. You'll end up seeing that it was worth it.

If you are out on a date night, consider sharing with your significant other. For the two of you, just order one dinner to share. Portion sizes at restaurants can be huge with a capital *H*. Just ask the server for an extra plate when the meal comes. Most restaurants these days are happy to have your business and will be glad to bring you an extra plate at no charge. If you do happen to have leftovers, bring them home. That will give you a free lunch the next day.

Ordering up

If you are eating out at a fast food chain, be careful when servers ask if you would like a larger size or additional toppings. Most of these things are not free but will be added to your total bill. Always ask if the up-sell is free. Skipping out on the larger size means fewer calories. You are already eating out, which means you will typically consume more calories than if you ate at home, so stick to the regular size and save money and your waistline!

Leftovers

Can't finish your food? No worries. Ask for a takeout box. Taking your unfinished food home will allow you to have a free lunch later on in the week. Two meals for the price of one.

Double Check the Check

Don't forget to check your receipt. This is important. Accidents happen. You don't want to pay for something that you didn't order. You also should be honest and let your server know if they forgot something. Check your receipts for any deals or coupons for your next visit. Some places offer free meals or a reward if you take a survey about your dining-out experience. Your experience should be fun and affordable. With a little planning and restraint, dining out can always be special.

Don't Forget the Tip

It is important to not forget to include a tip in your eating-out budget. I grew up with a grandfather who was a big tipper. He always told me to never forget the tip. We should always be appreciative of the men and women serving us our food and cleaning up after we leave a restaurant. My father now carries on this tradition. This type of thinking has stuck with me, and I always include tipping in my budget. A standard tip is

10–15 percent of whatever the total bill is. If you received above-average service, then tip accordingly. Whatever it is that you like to tip, make sure you include that in your budget.

Take the Kids

I know that all of us moms and dads want a night out every once and a while. We love our little munchkins, but sometimes it is nice to have a night out where family food fights and messy tables are not on the agenda. Although that night out is welcoming now and then, there are also some great benefits to taking the kids with you. Kids are messy. It happens. So you can have a night off from that messy table clean up but still get quality family time together. Another thing to think about is that the price of a kid's meal is often cheaper than a babysitter. Make it a family event. Check out your local restaurants and see which days are kids-eat-free nights.

Have Fun

This has got to be the *most* important one. When you are going out with the family, enjoy it! Put down the phones and talk. Unplug yourself and focus on the time spent with those you love. Giggle, joke, people watch (does anyone else do this?), tell stories . . . you get the gist. Just have fun being with your family.

If you can, make reservations. This cuts down on waiting and hunger time at the restaurant, which will save you money and calories in the end. No one likes waiting forever and a day for a table. Taking a bit of time beforehand to plan makes a huge difference when your relaxing night out comes up.

Chapter 11

A Clean Home Is a Happy Home

I am like any other mama out there who loves to have a clean house but finds it difficult to achieve this with little ones and a hubby. I love them, but they can make it difficult to keep a home organized. As a newly married couple, I found that things were pretty easy to keep organized and tidy. That was until we decided to throw two redheads into the mix. In late 2004, we welcomed our sweet little Keagan to our family. After the delivery, we moved to Washington and set up house. Hubby was in the military, and we were enjoying life living off-post. Three years later, we welcomed another redhead to our brood. Elizabeth joined our family in 2007. With two little munchkins to care for, I now had quite a task keeping up with housework. Between nursing a new baby and running after a toddler, I was having trouble making sure I showered every day, let alone mopped my floor. For the first time in my life, I understood what all those mamas had been telling me in my early twenties. I took back all those snarky comments I had made in my head because I now knew just how challenging keeping up with a house and kids could be.

I remember my husband coming home from work one day and finding me still in my pajamas. I hadn't even brushed my teeth yet. While my son played in the hall and my daughter napped, I was scrubbing a bathroom toilet. We were having company over that night, and I had convinced myself that I had to have my house completely perfect before anyone came over. Hubby took one look at me, in my sad, sad state, and told me to go shower. He grabbed that cleaning cloth from my hand and told me he would finish. Later that night, after our company had left and the dishes were cleaned, Hubby and I had a talk. I had been running myself ragged trying to create this picture-perfect life and home. I was driving myself bananas, and I think I was driving Hubby a bit bananas as well. I would get upset if he came home and didn't put his boots away immediately. I was becoming a drill sergeant, and because he followed orders all day, he preferred not to do it when he came home too. We needed a compromise. I still felt strongly that we should have a clean, tidy house, but I agreed that it did not have to be magazine-worthy every second.

We each talked about what we wanted our home to be. We agreed that our home should be a retreat from the world for our family. Our home should be a place of refuge. I needed to figure out how to do that without completely exhausting myself and without nagging my husband to death. I needed to set realistic expectations for myself, and I needed a hubby who would back me up when it was needed. We talked for a long time that night, and we finally came up with a plan. If I needed help with something, I had to speak up. I couldn't just assume that Hubby would notice that the dishes in the sink had to be washed or the shelves needed to be dusted. If I wanted help, I had to be specific about what I needed help with. Did he clean the bathroom the way I would have? Absolutely not. But finally, I was no longer alone in this cleaning battle. I had a partner who was helping me. That was such an encouragement.

I also started getting my little boy involved in the cleaning. Keagan was a little guy, but he could still help me around the house. I made it a fun thing that we did together. He would help me load the washer and then pull clothes out of the dryer. He even helped me clean the table. I would spray the table with homemade cleaner and then he would wipe it with a cloth. Did he do it perfectly? No, but he did what his three-year-old self could. I slowly realized that I would rather be a relaxed mama spending time with her children than a grumpy mama who was putting cleaning before her kids.

As my children have grown older, they have continued to help and are learning how to make a house a home. They are accepting responsibility and are helping in ways that are age-appropriate. I am so thankful for this. Once the whole family is included in the cleaning, things become a whole lot easier.

Cleaning the Home Is a Family Affair

By teaching our children at a young age to work hard and appreciate one another's efforts, we have made chores and cleaning part of our everyday lifestyle. We believe that because everyone lives in our home and contributes to the mess, then everyone should contribute to the cleanup. We are firm believers that a clean home is a happy home. We blare our favorite tunes from the speakers and get our clean on. We enjoy some times more than others, but no matter what, we do it as family. It has become a time that we laugh, joke, and—of course—clean.

Set a Time Frame

When you are having your children or husband do chores, it may help to set up a time frame for a given chore's completion. I learned the importance of this early in my marriage. When Hubby and I were first married, we decided that we would share the chores. I was a full-time college student, and he worked for a cable company. He was gone most of the day, while I was enrolled in online classes. We agreed that because I was at home, I would take care of most of the cleaning in the apartment and he would take care of the bathroom. He knew how much I hated cleaning bathrooms. (I still do.) After living there for six months, he never once cleaned the bathroom. When I asked him why, he sweetly replied, "You never told me *when* I had to do it." He cleaned that bathroom to get our cleaning deposit back when we moved out, and that was the only time he did it. I have since learned that Hubby does well with deadlines. If I want him to help me with a chore, I give him a deadline. Instead of, "Will you please clean the shower?" I ask, "Will you please clean the shower by Friday?" It does wonders.

Finish and Report Back

Once a chore is finished, we encourage our littles to come back and tell us that they are done. This is a way for them to be accountable for what they have done. It's a great way to know how much effort they actually put into a job. (They are a little hesitant to report back when they know they haven't given the job 100 percent effort, and they're excited to report when a job is done well.) We have found that this is a great way to teach our children how to follow through with tasks.

As we work as a family, we remind the littles that we are all working together. No one does the same job every day. Each member of the family does different jobs, which are appropriate for their ages. We all contribute to the mess, so we must all contribute to the cleaning.

Make Cleaning Fun

Turn on the music (add a cleaning playlist to your phone) or make cleaning a race. (Set a timer to see who can clean up the living room the quickest.) This is a great activity when a room needs to be picked up quickly. I have raised some competitive kids who take after their mama, so cleaning to the finish is always a hit. Make working together fun for your family.

Delegating Work and Responsibility to Children

Often, young mothers believe that picking up after their children and doing all the housework themselves is the only way to establish an orderly house. They tell themselves that they want their children to have a well-kept home, even it if means they have to do all the work. There is a big flaw in this line of thinking. Usually the mother is overworked and tired, while the child is left feeling indulged and entitled.

Learning to delegate work has been quite a struggle for me. I have always had the mentality that I will get things done quicker if I do them myself. I was always that kid in school who was the leader of the group projects and did most of the work. I always feared that someone would drop the ball or the project would be completed but not exactly the way I had envisioned in my head. I wanted that good grade and was willing to do most of the work just so I could achieve that A. When my kids were little and would ask to help me, I would tell them no because I felt that I could do it much faster and better on my own. One day, I had a change of heart. I realized that I was doing a disservice to my children. I was preventing them from having the gratification of knowing they did a job well.

There is an old saying: "A lazy mom does it herself." Children love to feel needed. They love to help mom put clothes in the washer or turn the light off for dad. They innately want to serve and help. Little by little, I started letting my kids help. I learned how to delegate. I had to let go of

> Reader's Question: How do you get your family involved in the household chores?
>
> "My daughter just turned two. She loves helping me tidy up the living room, fold clothes, do the dishes [and so on]. Most times she makes a bigger mess for me to clean up, but I figure if we make it fun now it won't seem so much as a chore later. I try to get her to 'help' me daily, even if it's just putting something away for me. She loves all the cheering she gets afterward."
>
> —*Amanda*

that control. I couldn't micromanage everything that happened in my home. I had to relax and just enjoy being a mom and wife.

When I take the time to teach them how to do work properly, they learn a lesson. They learn that a certain level of quality is expected. They learn that if that level is not reached, then they may have to redo it. These are things that happen in real life. If you had a presentation due at work and you did not complete it to your boss's specifications, you would have to redo it. Asking our children to redo those chores they slacked on prepares them for times in their lives when more will be expected of them. If they learn at a young age, then they will be prepared for when bigger things are asked of them. In the real world, no one is going to come save you if you fail to do your job. There are consequences to our actions. So if we teach our children to have pride in their work and be accountable for the little things, then they will be able to do greater things later on. We are shaping these little hearts we have been entrusted with. We want to prepare our children to be contributing members of society, so we must teach them at a young age that hard work is expected.

How to Delegate Work and Responsibility to Our Littles

David O. McKay said, "The privilege to work is a gift, the power to work is a blessing, the love of work is success."[1] What a beautiful message we can teach our children. When we are effective in our family leadership and in teaching our children these crucial lessons, we can bring about a balance between independence and responsibility. Through a few simple steps, we can delegate work and responsibility to our little ones and prepare them to work hard.

Determine the Chore

When deciding what chore to give your little ones, make sure that it is age-appropriate. When my kids were toddlers, I didn't have them clean the toilet. Instead, I assigned chores like wiping the table after dinner or helping put dishes in the dishwasher. As they got older, they could do harder tasks like mopping, vacuuming, and dusting.

Explain Clearly What Is Expected

I once asked my son to clean the bathroom counter for a daily chore. Once he was finished and ready for his work to be checked, I came in to find he had only cleaned around things. He had not moved one item off the counter to clean. When I chastised him for not doing that, he replied, "But you didn't tell me I had to move anything." When we ask our children to do a job, they need a clear understanding of our expectations. They need to know how we want the job done and what the end result should be. Because I didn't tell him to remove everything from the counter before cleaning, he didn't know that was necessary to finish the job to my specifications. Taking a bit more time now to teach them means we will have to take less time later.

Get a Commitment

Once we have given our children an assignment and we have explained what is expected, we now must get a commitment from them to complete the task. This is to make sure they understand what the chore is and what is expected. It makes them accountable for the task they will be performing. By inviting their responses, we can also discover and resolve any misunderstandings about the assignment. Furthermore, we are showing them that their response matters to us and is important. We are giving them a chance to deal with any feelings of inadequacy they may have about the job they have been given. Sometimes my children let me know how much they really don't want to do a chore I have asked them to complete. Kids are good about that. If they don't want to do something, they are quick to say so—sometimes in colorful ways. In such times, our children just need a bit of kind nudging from Mom and Dad. Reminding them that they are part of the family and that we are thankful for their help goes a long way to helping them feel better about contributing.

Give Training with Love and Encouragement

Loving encouragement and patient repetition are necessary to develop responsibility in our children. Children learn by repetition, just like we do. Sometimes we need to be told something over and over again so we understand what is going on. Learning does not always occur the first time, nor perhaps even the first dozen times. Children usually have short attention spans, so they need short, simple directions. This is something I remind myself of often. This prevents me from overwhelming my kids with my explanations. I also ask them, "Do you understand?" This is a great way to give them an opportunity to ask for clarification if it is needed.

If a child does not complete a task, we must resist the urge to take over the responsibility. In a firm but calm voice we must remind our

> *"We don't call them 'chores,' we call them their 'family contribution.' It's expected that they contribute to our family by helping clean our home. We don't pay them for their regular 'lists' (we do have a list of extra things they can do to earn money after their regular stuff is done). My motivators are to work with them, praise them, have them teach another sibling how to do a chore, and help them to feel the gratification in a job well done. I am always telling them that we are happier when we are working hard; our spirits love to work, but it's the 'natural man' that is lazy. Teaching them to work in the home prepares them for having their own families and serving missions and succeeding in college. It's super important, so it's a big focus in our family."*
>
> *—Allison*

children to do what was asked of them. When my kids are having trouble getting work done due to distractions, we remind them that if the chores do not get done, then they don't get to play. Usually a simple reminder is enough to get their motors running again.

Cleaning the home can certainly be a challenge, depending on how many are in your family. No matter your family size though, there is a way to do it and still keep a peaceful feeling in your home. Make it fun and enjoy that time together, making it a learning opportunity, and never forget that pat on the back and the "You did a great job!" It truly makes a difference.

Cleaning the Homemade Way

I have a confession for you all. I have a thing for good smells; great cologne, home-baked bread, and scented candles are some of my favorites.

Before I started my frugal journey, I would spend hundreds of dollars a year trying out all those smell-good products in the home cleaning section at the grocery store. My cabinets were overflowing with different fragrances and bottles that I had tried. When we finally started our frugal journey and I realized the way I shopped had to change, I knew my obsession with smells had to be reined in as well. I could no longer afford to try one of everything in the Home and Cleaning Section just because a product had a sticker that said it was new. I soon realized that I could save my family precious dollars by making stuff at home, with items I already had in my pantry. By using items like baking soda, vinegar, bar soap, and water, I was able to make a lot of cleaners for pennies that my family uses every day!

Once I made my first bottle of homemade cleaner, I was hooked. Here are my family's basic cleaning recipes. I have a great distaste for the smell of vinegar, but it makes a perfect, budget-friendly cleaner. My solution is essential oils. Add a few drops of your favorite essential oil to cover up the vinegar smell in homemade cleaners. (My favorite essential oils are lemon grass, tee tree oil, orange, and lavender.)

I love using these cleaners in my home, and I hope you too will see how simple, inexpensive, and fun it is to make these imitations of store-bought cleaners. These are nontoxic and perfect when little hands and big hands are helping. You too can have a clean home without the chemicals or the cost!

Fabric Freshener Spray
    funnel
    tablespoon
    fabric softener
    hot water
    empty spray bottle (32 oz.)

Using your funnel, pour three tablespoons of fabric softener into your empty spray bottle. Next, fill the bottle up the rest of the way with hot water from the faucet. Once your bottle is filled with water, give it a good shake to mix the contents. Label your bottle. Use this fabric spray to freshen all your fabrics and rugs.

All-Purpose Cleaner
    funnel
    1 cup white distilled vinegar
    3 cups water
    10 drops of essential oil
    empty spray bottle (32 oz.)

Using the funnel, fill your empty bottle with the vinegar. Next, add your water and essential oil. Put the nozzle on your bottle and shake to mix contents together. Don't forget to give your bottle a label too! I use this cleaner for my kitchen counters, stove top, bathroom counters, kitchen table, and mirrors. It really is an all-purpose cleaner.

Orange Citrus Cleaner
    1–2 quart-size mason jars
    orange, grapefruit, or lemon peels

white distilled vinegar
empty spray bottle (32 oz.)

Fill your quart jars about half full of citrus peels. Feel free to pack them in there. Fill the jars the rest of the way with vinegar. Cover tightly with a lid, give it a good shake, and then write the date on the top so you don't forget!

Allow the peels and vinegar to steep for about two weeks. The longer it sits, the more potent it will get. After time has elapsed, place the mixture in a blender. Blend until peels are completely combined with vinegar. Your mixture will basically look like orange juice now. Strain your orange mixture through a piece of cheesecloth to remove any lingering bits of orange peel pulp. Throw out the pulp and place your orange mixture back into Mason jars for storage. Label your jars. When using your citrus cleaner, dilute 1:1 with water (one part citrus vinegar to one part water) and place in your spray bottle. Use as an all-purpose cleaner for toilets, counters, and so on.

Laundry Detergent
    3 bars of Ivory soap
    5-gallon storage bucket
    4 lb. box of baking soda
    4 lb. box of borax
    4 lb. box of super washing soda

Using a cheese grater or food processor with the grater attachment on, grate your soap. Place your soap into a 5-gallon storage bucket. We use the storage buckets sold at home improvement stores. Once you've added your grated soap, add the remaining ingredients to the bucket. Combine all ingredients in the bucket and mix well. For finely grated powder laundry detergent, I like to give the soap mixture another round through my food processor. I put the blade attachment on and run all the detergent through the food processor in batches. This is will give you a fine laundry detergent powder. Use ⅓ cup for one load of laundry.

NOTES

1. David O. McKay, *Pathways to Happiness* (Salt Lake City, UT: Deseret Book, 1957), 381.

Chapter 12

Keep Calm and Carry On

This chapter is full of those last few thoughts I want to share with you. I have given you a lot of information in this book—information that can truly bless your family, if you allow it to. I want you to know that I have been where you are. I remember being that girl, not knowing how she would climb out of the financial hole she was in. I remember feeling overwhelmed and discouraged. I remember listening to the naysayers telling me it was too hard. I want you to know that you can do this. You can do hard things. This book has been my baby for the past year. I have prayed and thought about what should be put into it. I want you to know that I truly believe in frugal living, with every fiber of my being. I have seen it do amazing things in my life. I have seen it do amazing things in the lives of those I teach to budget.

Before I end this book, I want to leave you with a few last thoughts on keeping on for the long haul and making those financial goals. Through a changed mind-set, making lasting habits, and celebrating the small victories, you will be able to succeed on this frugal journey you are beginning. No matter what, know that you can do this. I believe in you! I am there right along with you, cheering you on. You've got this!

A Changed Mind-Set

As I have traveled down this road of frugal living, I have learned an important lesson: if I want to succeed in learning to live a different way, then I need to change the way I think about things. The way you were raised or the circumstances you are currently in cannot be an excuse for

139

the way that you behave with your finances. You have a choice in what you are doing. When I had buried myself in debt, I had no one to blame but myself. No one made me take all those trips to the store; I did it on my own accord. Whatever situation you are in, own it. Don't enshroud yourself in excuses. I did this for a long time, and it didn't make things better. In fact, things only got worse. Our attitude can greatly affect the way we look at the world around us. Our attitude and the way we look at things really can make or break us. If we look at our financial situation as a challenge and an opportunity to discover new opportunities for our-selves, it will become a game. We will no longer look at what has become of our finances with disdain. We will finally see hope where before there was none.

No matter your financial situation, know that you have a say in what is going on in your life. If you are unhappy with where you are right now, start making changes. You can't do it overnight, but you can make things better. Developing a frugal mind-set takes time. We must be patient with ourselves. Whenever I work with a new couple, and we've just made a budget for their family, I always ask them one question. "Are you good?" This is my way of asking if they have any questions or are feeling over-whelmed. I usually receive a big sigh and a smile, followed by "I think so." It is at this moment that I like to remind them that they are better off than they were yesterday because today they have a plan. A well-thought-out plan will make all the difference. Never forget that. Right now, today, you are better off than you were yesterday because you have a desire to change your life. That is a big deal. Give yourself a pat on the back. You rock!

When I started making a change in my own life, I realized early on that the first thing that had to change was me. All the best intentions were great, but if I didn't change the way I looked at things and behaved, then my family would not be able to have a financially secure future. I had to change my mind-set. Thinking differently can change everything. It reminds me of what happens when you look at a piece of art. Some see beauty, and others only see lines on canvas. As time goes on and you gain experience, you may see a little bit more in that painting. You may start to feel what the artist felt as they created that beautiful work of art. This is similar to our own lives. We may be frustrated or upset with what is going on in our lives. We may be looking at our finances in a negative light. We are only seeing the lines in the canvas, but as we gain knowl-edge and experience in this frugal journey, we will notice a huge change taking place. All of a sudden, those lines are changing. We are starting to see that beauty. We will start to see how all of our planning and saving is making things better. It will take time, but it can happen for each and every one of us.

For so long, I was used to getting anything I wanted. When I got married and things started to change, I didn't understand why my spending habits had to change as well. When I looked at my life, I was yet again only seeing the lines on the canvas. As I applied the tips in this book into my own life, I started to realize something. I started to realize that it all came down to one essential line of thought: either we control our finances or our finances control us.

Changing your mind-set and attitude is a gradual process. It happens line upon line, precept upon precept. Allow yourself a little grace as you learn. If you slip up, dust yourself off and try again. I know it takes a bit of work to take control of our finances, but if we don't do it, who will?

Make Lasting Habits

Once you set a budget and begin to change your attitude, you have to begin making lasting habits as well. All the best-planned-out budgets will not make much of an impact unless you change your habits. I have witnessed countless families who work tirelessly to get themselves out of debt, only to find themselves back in their same position a year later. They work so hard to pay off their debt, but they don't change the habits that landed them in that debt to begin with. Making lasting habits will allow you to get out of debt and stay out of debt.

I have discovered that making lasting habits is a slow process. It takes time for these to develop. When you are beginning to develop a new habit, it is usually after the realization that there may be a better way to do what you are currently doing. That is what happened to me. I had hit rock bottom, realizing that my way of money management didn't work for my family. I didn't think life had to be so hard. It is sometimes a humbling thing to admit that what you are doing is not working out the way that you would like. So you do a bit of research, and when you find a new way to do it, you try it out. Once you have repeated that new way enough times, it will become a habit.

Start off slow. It is similar to when you learn a new dance. At first you are unsure of the moves, but as you practice them over and over again, muscle memory starts to kick in. You can do them without much thought. This is what happens as you learn to live frugally. I remember when we first started out, I had become so accustomed to shopping that I needed a bit of a detox. If I went into certain stores, I was bound to spend money. Because of this, I had to keep away. For a while I steered clear of these stores. I needed to gain my own self-control before I could go back to those places. This is very similar to when I had to lock my credit cards away. I did this to help myself be able to make new habits.

Being aware of what your triggers are will help. I know that for me, I will turn to shopping when things feel out of my control. If you are a shopaholic, you may always have those tendencies to shop. Whether you give in to that temptation is up to you. I think back to when my brother passed away. It was very sudden and understandably made me feel as if I had no control. As I grieved over that loss, I found myself wanting to walk around some of my favorite stores more and more. Because I know that this is something I tend to do, I was able to nip it in the bud. Instead of heading to the store to escape the feelings of great sadness I was enduring, I found other ways to fill my time. I read books, went for walks with my family, and had a lot of movie marathons with the kids. I was able to find another way to deal with what was going on in my life. Because I had made a habit to not go shopping anytime life wasn't going my way, I was able to prevent myself from going into debt when my family suffered a great loss.

Celebrate the Small Victories

When I am teaching people about budgeting, I always encourage them to celebrate the small victories. Celebrating does not mean going out to eat or on a shopping spree. That used to be how I celebrated. I learned that I didn't need to spend money to make things special. A lot of times, Hubby and I will chat about how things are going. When we pay off a bill (like our son's braces) or we find that we have saved up enough money for something we have been wanting, we celebrate. We give each other little pats on the pack and do our own little happy dances. It is important to celebrate those small victories because all the small things we do each day add up to really big things.

I remember when our son needed braces. He has a speech impediment and really needed those braces to help him with his speech. We saved for a down payment, and then he got his braces. We had sixteen months to pay off the rest of the braces. Sixteen months was too long for us. We decided to up our monthly payments so we could pay them off sooner. Each month, when a payment was sent in, we would celebrate that total going down. Eventually we were able to send in that last payment six months ahead of schedule. What a wonderful moment that was.

I encourage you today to know how amazing you are. Know that you can do this. The world may try to convince you that it is too hard to embrace a frugal lifestyle or that you will be missing out on so much if you do, but I want to set the record straight, lovelies. Living below your means and embracing the frugal lifestyle will allow you to take back your financial freedom. Working to avoid or eliminate your debt will help to reduce stress and increase a feeling of peace into your home. Remember that *no debt is too great.* Keep calm and carry on. You've got this!

Testimonials

"Danielle's frugal tips truly have changed my life. She makes frugality fun and effective!"
—Cate (Everly, IA)

"You have changed my outlook on life and my financial situation. When I first quit my full-time job to be a more involved mom, I was scared that I had made the wrong decision. I now see myself free from the material ambitious I had and more . . . the woman God called me to be. Yes, I am broke and I have to cut many corners, but I would not trade my life for anything. I am very happy.) You were the first person that made me proud of making ends meet. I left my job and my career in the fashion industry. I am now a part-time teacher's aide and full-time mom. That is the way I like it! Seeing that I am not alone makes me feel better and encouraged to keep on going."
—Elizabeth (San Bernardino, CA)

"My name is Jean, and I just wanted to say thank you for all of the time and thought you put into your blog. I found your blog about a year and a half ago through Pinterest (isn't Pinterest the best?) and have been reading it since. Over that year and a half, my husband and I have welcomed our first child into the world, and I went from teaching third grade to being a stay-at-home mom. With that change came a budget shift, and your blog has provided countless tips and tricks for our family to save money, especially at the grocery store. You have taught me to create a meal plan and cut out all of those last-minute runs to the grocery store. You have helped change my thought process about spending money, and now I really do think about every penny we spend. Thank you for sharing recipes, homeschooling stories, menu plans, budgeting tips, crafts, and your love of Jesus."
—Jean B. (Rosharon, TX)

About the Author

Danielle is a self-proclaimed budgeting diva who has learned through her own experience how to make frugal living work. She started her blog, *Blissful and Domestic*, in 2009 as a way to document her frugal journey. Little did she know it would turn into a labor of love where she daily shares tips and tricks to help people learn to create a beautiful life on less. She continues to share this knowledge through teaching others how to ~~dget~~ in her community and at church. She lives in Las Vegas, Nevada, ~~her~~ hubby and two redheads.